FROM WAR TO WEALTH
FIFTY YEARS OF INNOVATION

Scott Sullivan

ORGANISATION FOR ECONOMIC CO-OPERATION AND DEVELOPMENT

PHOTOS CREDITS

Cover: **SERGE ATTAL** (top), **PAUL ALMASY** (bottom).

Chapter **I**
OECD/OCDE: Daniel White.

Chapter **II**
OECD/OCDE & USIS/ECA/OECD/OCDE: pp. 9, 10, 11 (centre), 12, 15, 17 (bottom), 20, 21, 22, 23, 24, 25, 26, 27. **KEYSTONE:** pp. 11 (top & bottom), 13, 16,17 (top), 18. **Anne de Speth:** pp. 20, 21. **FIAT & Compagnie Nationale du Rhône:** p. 27.

Chapter **III**
SYGMA: pp. 28: Régis Bossu, 36 (top), 43: J.-P. Laffont; p. 41 (top): Atlan; p. 41 (bottom): D. Hudson; p. 44: Alain Nogues; p. 45 (bottom): Les Stone. **OECD/OCDE:** p. 30; p. 31 (top): Eddy van der Veen; pp. 31 (bottom), 42, 45 (top): Leo Jouan; pp. 34 (bottom), 37 (left), 38 (top): Sabine Weiss; p. 46 (centre): Claude Stefan; (bottom): Darryl Evans. **USIS/OECD/OCDE:** p. 32. **MAGNUM/ René Burri:** p. 35. **KEYSTONE:** pp. 36, 39 (bottom). **NEWSWEEK:** p. 39 (centre). **GAMMA:** p. 37 (bottom): Francolon; p. 39 (top): Chip Hires. **RAPHO:** p. 38 (bottom): Cagnoni. **EDF:** p. 40. **SERGE ATTAL:** p. 42 (top). **REA:** p. 42 (bottom): Saba/Carter.

Chapter **IV**
SYGMA: pp. 47, 51 (bottom right): Bernard Annebicque; p. 51 (top left): Frederic Pitchal; p. 51 (top right): Régis Bossu; p. 53: Gérard Rancinan; p. 54: APN. **OECD/OCDE:** p. 48: Peter Paul; p. 49: Heinz Wedewardt; pp. 50 (top), 52, 55, 62: Leo Jouan; p. 56, 60: Silvia Thompson; pp. 53 (centre), 57 (top), 62: Daniel White; pp. 57, 58 (bottom): OECD/OCDE; p. 61: Leo Jouan, Daniel White, Claude Stefan, Darryl Evans; p. 63: Leo Jouan, Brigitte Cavanagh. **REA:** p. 50: C. Boisseau-Chical/La Vie; p. 51 (bottom left): Saba/Resnick; p. 53 (bottom left): Renato Assis; p. 57 (top): Allard; p. 57 (bottom): Jean Pottier; p. 58: Saba/ T. Wagner; p. 59 (bottom): Saba/R. Wallis. **SERGE ATTAL:** p. 59 (top). **RHÔNE-POULENC:** p. 59 (centre).

Chapter **V**
OECD/OCDE: Leo Jouan, Claude Stefan, G. McInnes, Darryl Evans, Silvia Thompson, Bobbie Kingsley, Sabine Weiss, Peter Paul, Peter Turnley. **ROGER VIOLLET:** p. 10 (top). **RAPHO/REFOT:** p. 22 (centre).

Chapter **VI**
PASCALE LARIVIERE: p. 85. **ILO/BIT:** p. 87 (top). **RAPHO:** p. 87 (bottom): Valérie Winckler; p. 93 (top): D. Dailloux; (centre): Hervé Donnezan; (bottom): George Gerster. **SYGMA:** p. 88 (top): J.-P. Laffont; (bottom): Stéphane Compoint; p. 89 (bottom): Alain Nogues; p. 92 (top)J-P Amet. **REA:** p. 89 (top): Saba/Edinger; p. 95: Leimdorfer; p. 97 (top): van Cappellen; (centre): Doumic. **OECD/OCDE:** p. 90: Daniel White; pp. 92, 101 (top): Silvia Thompson; pp. 98, 99: Daniel White, Willy Braga, Claude Stefan; **KIPA:** p. 94. **ESA:** p. 96. **HOA QUI:** p. 97 (bottom). **SERGE ATTAL:** pp. 100, 101 (bottom).

Chapter **VII**
UNITED COLOURS OF BENNETON: p. 103: Oliviero Toscani. **OECD/OCDE:** pp. 104, 114: Darryl Evans; pp. 105, 114: Leo Jouan; pp. 110, 112: Claude Stefan; p. 111: Daniel White; p. 113: Dominique Berretty; p. 114: Sabine Weiss. **KEYSTONE:** p. 106. **RAPHO:** p. 107 (top): Hervé Donnezan. **SERGE ATTAL:** p. 107 (bottom). **REA:** p. 108: Benoît Decout. **ROGER VIOLLET:** p. 109.

CONTENTS

Chapter I

Fifty Years
and
Going Strong

Fifty Years
and Going Strong

THIS is a birthday book: the birthday book of an idea.

That idea – dazzling in its simplicity, epoch-making in its reach – was the concept of co-operation. Co-operation among proud and self-regarding nation-states. Co-operation between traditional enemies. Co-operation to be built out of the ashes of a cataclysmic war. If only, the fathers of the idea argued, the knowledge and the energies of the warring nations could be harnessed to a common project, they might achieve such progress as the world had never known. The stakes were high, the chances of success uncertain. But the goal was so compelling that the idea *must* be made to work.

Like all great ideas, this one had several fathers. Franklin Roosevelt, and Winston Churchill used it as the cornerstone of the Atlantic Charter, then of the United Nations. Konrad Adenauer and Charles de Gaulle built a new relationship between their alienated peoples upon it. Robert Schuman, Jean Monnet and Alcide de Gasperi applied it to the organisation now known as the European Union. The authors of the Bretton Woods accords gave it a monetary and financial expression. It sparked the creation of the General Agreement on Tariffs and Trade, now the World Trade Organisation.

Nowhere, however, did the notion of international co-operation receive clearer or more urgent expression than in the plan for European reconstruction announced by George Marshall at Harvard University in 1947 – just a half-century ago. Not only, Marshall said, would the United States contribute of its riches to rebuild the shattered economies of Europe. The aid would be contingent on the Europeans' willingness to co-operate among themselves: in sharing out the Marshall Plan money; in demolishing the protectionist trade barriers among them; in finding a way to exchange their non-convertible currencies efficiently.

Amazingly, the idea worked. Success came rapidly and it exceeded even the wildest hopes of its proponents. Well within a decade, Europe had reached and surpassed its pre-war levels of production and prosperity. Marshall Plan aid ended, but the idea remained as vibrant as ever. The organisation that Marshall recipients had formed to administer American largesse expanded to include the United States and Canada, and not long after, Japan. Co-operation took new forms, expanded, institutionalised.

OECD – the Organisation for Economic Co-operation and Development – is the continuing embodiment of George Marshall's idea. A permanent meeting-place for democratic nations with market economies, 29 of them now. A laboratory of policy concepts in areas as diverse as export credits, corporate governance and the control of pornography on the Internet. A pool of statistical and economic expertise for its members. A beacon of freedom and accomplishment for the rest of the world.

This, then, is the birthday book of an idea and of an institution: the idea of co-operation and the Organisation that incarnates it.

Birthdays are times to look back at beginnings. Few stories are as dramatic as the birthing time of the Marshall Plan and of the Organisation for European Economic Co-operation, which was created to manage it. Europe was a smoking battlefield over which some 25 million refugees wandered. Guerrilla warfare in Greece foreshadowed what was later to become the Cold War. The "experts" predicted the Continent would take decades to rebuild its shattered economies. But a small group of men, most of them in the American State Department, believed the vicious circle of war, poverty, nationalism and more war could be broken. Within a matter of weeks, they developed the outlines of the plan that Marshall would announce at Harvard. In Europe, men of similar vision – Ernest Bevin in England, Georges Bidault in France – leapt at the American suggestion. Within months, OEEC was operative, funds had been apportioned among countries which just recently had faced each other in a cruel war. The first shiploads of Marshall aid were soon unloaded at Le Havre and Bremen, and the miracle of postwar revival was under way.

Birthdays recall the critical moments of life. The first 20 years of the OEEC, then OECD, resemble an optimistic idyll, but the world later caught up with a vengeance. After almost two decades of unparalleled growth and booming trade, the Yom Kippur war of 1973 and the sudden quadrupling of oil prices faced the Western democracies with a daunting challenge. Wealth drained from them into the hands of the Organisation of Petroleum Exporting Countries. Recession threatened. Unemployment rose. There were two elements to dealing with the crisis. The OECD created a counter-OPEC, the International Energy Agency, charged with preparing the West for future "oil shocks". And it promoted the concept of "recycling petro-dollars" in order to return much of the money spent on more expensive oil to the consuming countries, whence it came. Ultimately, the two-pronged action overcame years of "stagflation" and left OECD countries armed against a further OPEC attack. They were, however, totally unprepared for the next great crisis of the half-century: the crumbling of Communism and the disappearance of the Soviet Union – events heartily to be wished but which threatened political and economic disruption around the world. Again, OECD and its members rose to a challenge, developed an impressive array of programmes to aid the newly democratising countries to deal with the endless problems of transition.

Birthdays recall growing up. Gradually, OECD grew, changed, adapted. Its economists and statisticians gained universal recognition for their constantly updated studies of the economies of member states, then of countries outside the Organisation, as well. The expansionist Keynesian economic model which had guided OECD through its first 20 years was amended, attacked and ultimately discarded for the supply-side approach. Although the Organisation's focus remained on macroeconomic policy, it delved deeper in a dozen different directions: education and the environment, science and technology, tax systems and development aid. With its relatively small staff – never more than 2 000 – it could take "horizontal" or "multi-disciplinary" approaches to policy issues.

Economists, computer scientists, and social policy and trade experts worked together on projects that ignored traditional scientific and bureaucratic boundaries. Despite its championing of structural reform and adaptation to new conditions, OECD increasingly concentrated on exploring the social difficulties and individual upheavals that such changes had in store.

Birthdays are about people. So is OECD. Indeed, the Organisation has only one resource: the wisdom and devotion of the men and women who serve its Secretariat and sit on its committees. So far, at least, they have never flagged. A day at "the Château" is a whirlwind of activity, a beehive of energy, a bubbling pot of ideas on every subject under the sun. It's well worth a visit.

Birthdays are about new as well as old things. Innovation has been the hallmark of OEEC-OECD since its first day. Indeed, its very foundation was an act of pioneering in itself. Nothing like it was to be found anywhere. For half a century, it has maintained the tradition, reforming and adapting itself time after time, striving to stay not only abreast but ahead of the mindstunning evolution of the modern world. It has blazed trails in both style and substance. It has developed a system at the interface between research and government that provides policy-makers with the very latest of academic thinking – and with a chance to thrash out difficulties together. It has come to serve as a proving ground for ideas that later emerge in WTO or the Group of Seven or, more simply, the legislatures of member countries. Many of the subjects now preoccupying the Organisation didn't exist a dozen years ago: cryptography, genetic engineering, intellectual property rights on the Internet. And there are subjects which exist largely because OECD detected a connection between apparently unrelated themes: trade and investment; development aid and the environment; tax collection and money-laundering.

Finally, birthdays are for looking forward. OECD faces serious new problems and enormous opportunities. Money is short, and competition from other organisations is growing. Some wonder whether an organisation as small as OECD can hope to master the complexities that lie ahead. Others foresee that, as the Organisation expands, it may lose focus and homogeneity. But Donald Johnston, the Secretary-General, has few doubts. He argues that the co-operative ideas embodied in the Marshall speech and the Marshall Plan are more relevant than ever today. The very fact of complexity makes OECD more important and useful than ever before. If international co-operation continues to win out over international hostility and national selfishness, Johnston predicts, "the sky's the limit". And those who work with him agree.

So, puff out the 50 candles, take a sip of champagne and spare a thought for the amazing saga that began at Harvard 50 years ago.

Happy birthday, OECD! And many happy returns!

Chapter II

Mister Marshall Changes the World

EUROPE
· ALL OUR COLOURS TO THE MAST ·

Winner OEEC poster competition, 1950, by Reijin Dirksen of the Netherlands

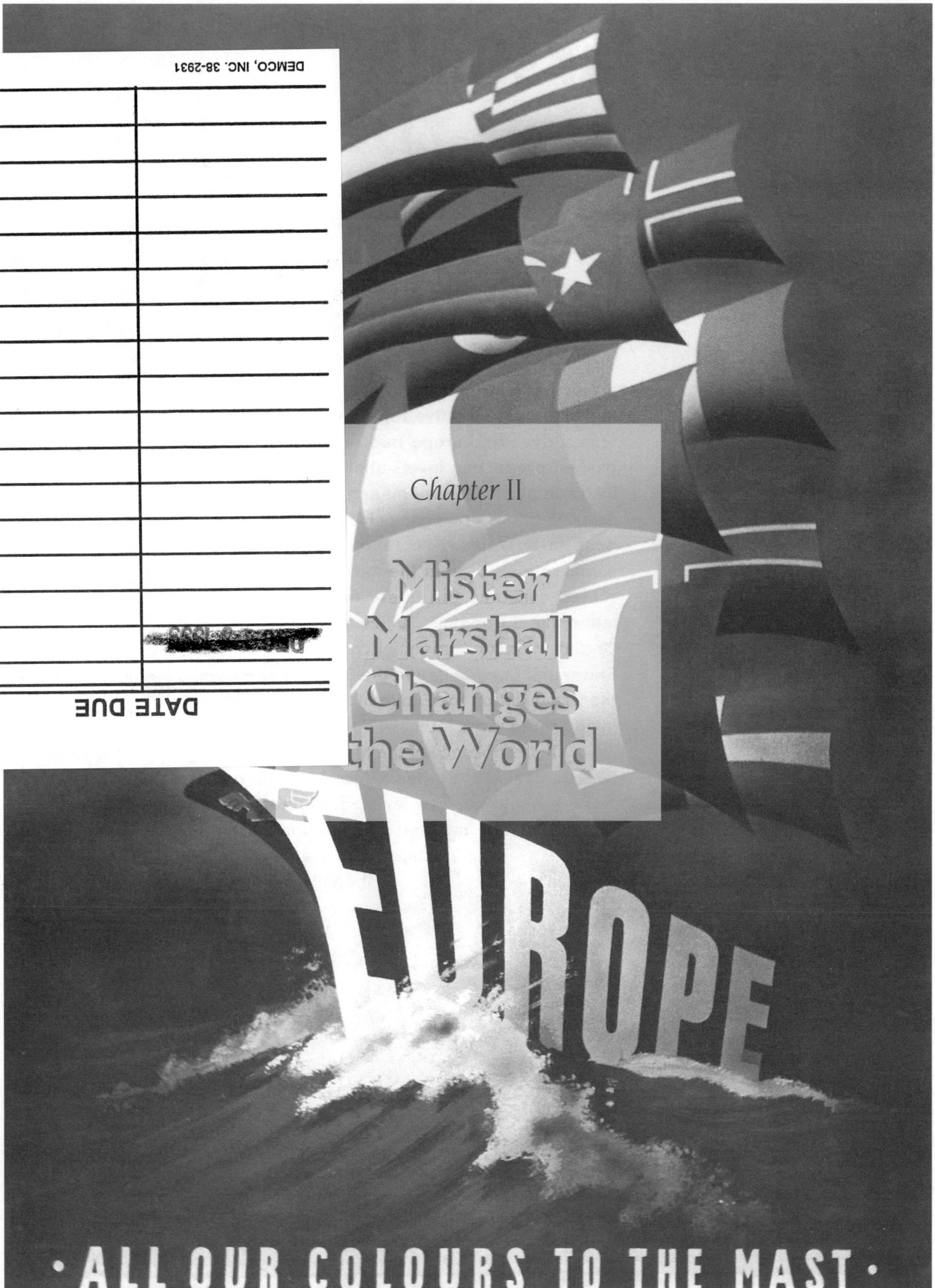

Mister Marshall
Changes the World

GEORGE **C. Marshall planted the seed. By a single act of inspired statesmanship, Marshall sparked the rapid reconstruction of Europe's war-devastated economies and initiated a process of international co-operation that continues to this day.**

The "Marshall Plan" for European recovery, announced in a short speech at Harvard University on 5 June, 1947, was arguably the most generous and the most effective foreign policy initiative in history. Within less than a decade, Europe had restored infrastructures and economies, pushed production levels above pre-war performance and multiplied its trade by an order of magnitude.

As a condition of receiving aid, the scholar-soldier who served as President Harry Truman's secretary of state, challenged European governments to look beyond the narrow concerns of the nation state to the shared concerns and interests of them all. In response to that challenge, the Europeans – allies and former enemies alike – created the Organisation for European Economic Co-operation. In 1961, the United States and Canada joined the OEEC members in a new grouping called the Organisation for Economic Co-operation and Development. Japan joined three years later.

In the absence of the Marshall Plan, Europe's return to normalcy could have taken a decade longer than it did. OEEC and OECD would not have existed. And the complex, innovative process of international co-operation that has animated so many busy days at the Château de la Muette might never have been begun.

US Secretary of State George C. Marshall entering Harvard University, 5 June, 1947

Anyone who had predicted in the spring of 1947 that Western Europe would soon embark on a half-century of unparalleled economic progress would have been regarded as raving mad.

Five years of savage warfare had shattered the Continent and Great Britain. Cities like Köln and Dresden, Coventry and Caen had been reduced to rubble. Highways, railroads and rolling stock, ocean harbours lay in ruins; in the areas of Eastern and Central Europe controlled by the Soviet Union, the occupying troops systematically plundered whatever of value

had survived the conflict. Twenty-five million Europeans had been forced to flee their homes; eleven million refugees from Central and Eastern Europe poured into Western Germany alone. In many regions, the male population between 20 and 30 years old had fallen by more than a quarter.

Industrial production had slowed to a trickle, less than two-thirds of pre-1940 norms in Austria, Greece and Italy. Not only had plants been destroyed or diverted to military production, but normal supplies of raw materials had dried up. Farmers had ceased bringing their produce to market in town; there were no manufactured goods to be bought for the money they might earn. Daily food rations in many cities fell to 1 000 calories a day, less than half the normal diet of an adult worker. Trade had diminished to a fraction of its pre-war level. Europe could no longer afford to buy food and raw materials from the rest of the world. Desperate governments, seeking to protect what remained of their national industries, slapped restrictions on imports, which were met by retaliatory trade constraints in a vicious and apparently unbreakable circle. In a situation of unstable exchange rates and with no central payment arrangements, Europe reverted to something like a barter system. Every European state laboured under a massive trade deficit that it had no means to finance – most of the mounting debt being owed to the United States. By 1947, the shortfall had reached $7 billion.

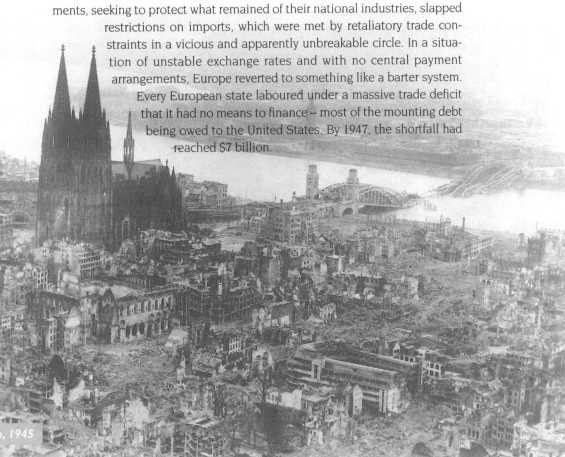

Köln, 1945

Political peril darkened the picture. Moscow was gobbling up one country after another in its postwar sphere of influence. In France and Italy, home-grown Communist parties were exploiting the intolerable living conditions in a bid for increased power and influence. In northern Greece, rebel forces with Communist backing were fighting a low-level war against the government in Athens.

Then came the disastrous winter of 1946-47, one of the longest and coldest in memory. Coalpits flooded and coal production was paralysed. Steel mills, crippled by lack of coal, produced barely half what they had before the war. Europeans shivered in their homes, offices and factories. Worse: the torrid summers of both 1946 and 1947 had slashed the grain harvest by half. In a radio broadcast on 28 April, 1947, Marshall described Europe as "crying out for help, for food, for most of the necessities of life… The patient is sinking while the doctors deliberate."

"The patient is sinking while the doctors deliberate"

In fact, the doctors were hard at work on both diagnosis and prescription. Marshall had gathered a small group of his closest advisers to work on a plan for Europe. It included Dean Acheson, then under-secretary of state, Will Clayton, assistant secretary for economic affairs and George Kennan, head of Marshall's own policy planning staff. "Avoid trivia!" was the Secretary's laconic warning.

They did. Within weeks, the special group had established the principles that would underlie the plan. Aid must be delivered quickly. It must be massive. It should advance

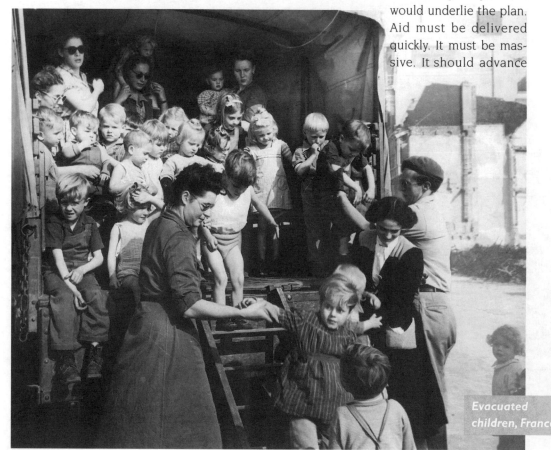

Evacuated children, France

not only European recovery but European integration. The Europeans should develop their own plan for dividing the aid among themselves. It should be offered to the whole of Europe, East and West.

This last point was the trickiest. Few American officials retained any illusions about the Soviet Union's expansionary aims. At the same time, Washington did not wish to be seen as excluding Central and Eastern Europe from the largesse it was about to bestow. In a lecture given during the drafting of the Marshall Plan, Kennan told students at the National War College: "It may be fairly stated as a working rule for dealing with the Russians that only those people are able to get along with them who have proven their ability to get along without them."

All those ideas were worked into the Harvard speech.

On 4 June, Marshall flew to Boston and spent the night at the home of James Conant, the president of Harvard. The following morning he received an honorary doctorate; also receiving honorary degrees were T.S. Eliot, General Omar Bradley and J. Robert Oppenheimer. After lunch, Marshall spoke before the Harvard Alumni Association.

The speech was short: six double-spaced pages. It opened with a powerful evocation of Europe's plight. It went on to explain America's double interest in helping out; along with the humanitarian impulse, the United States was interested in fostering "political and social conditions in which free institutions can exist". The secretary of state appealed to the American people to support a vast aid programme in "distant Europe". To the leaders of Western Europe, he issued a series of challenges. The initiative for the programme should come from them. They must agree among themselves on their needs and on how American aid should be divided.

Marshall offered Stalin's government a simple choice: to participate in the plan on a co-operative basis or to stay out altogether. "Any government," Marshall said, "that is willing to assist in the task of recovery will find full co-operation, I am sure, on the part of the United States Government. Any government which manœuvres to block the recovery of other countries cannot expect help from us. Furthermore, governments, political parties or groups which seek to perpetuate human misery in order to profit therefrom,

politically or otherwise, will encounter the opposition of the United States."

In the event, the Soviets passed up the American offer of aid. They also prevented their new satellites from joining in the plan; Czechoslovakia actually applied to participate, but quickly withdrew under pressure from Moscow. (Historians still quarrel over whether Marshall himself would have preferred to have the Russians in or out. The issue may never be resolved.)

MARSHALL'S HARVARD SPEECH

SECRETARY of State George C. Marshall's speech to the Harvard Alumni Association on 5 June, 1947, launched one of the most generous and effective foreign-policy initiatives in world history.

The main sections of the Marshall text:

"I need not tell you gentlemen that the world situation is very serious. That must be apparent to all intelligent people...

"In considering the requirements for the rehabilitation of Europe, the physical loss of life, the visible destruction of cities, factories, mines and railroads was correctly estimated, but [...] this visible destruction was probably less serious than the dislocation of the entire fabric of the European economy. For the past 10 years conditions have been highly abnormal. The feverish preparation for war and the more feverish maintenance of the war effort engulfed all aspects of national economies. Machinery has fallen into disrepair or is entirely obsolete. Under the arbitrary and destructive Nazi rule, virtually every possible enterprise was geared into the German war machine. Longstanding commercial ties, private institutions, banks, insurance companies and shipping companies disappeared, through loss of capital, absorption by nationalisation or by simple destruction. In many countries, confidence in the local currency has been severely shaken...

"The truth of the matter is that Europe's requirements for the next three or four years of foreign food and other essential products – principally from America – are so much greater than her ability to pay that she must have substantial additional help or face economic, social and political deterioration of a very grave character.

"The remedy seems to lie in breaking the vicious circle and restoring the confidence of the people of Europe in the economic future of their own countries and of Europe as a whole. The manufacturer and the farmer throughout wide areas must be able and willing to exchange their products for currencies the continuing value of which is not open to question...

"It is logical that the United States should do whatever it is able to do to assist the return of normal economic health in the world, without which there can be no political stability and no assured peace. Our policy is directed not against any country or doctrine but against hunger, poverty, desperation and chaos. Its purpose should be the revival of a working economy in the world so as to permit the emergence of political and social conditions in which free institutions can exist. Such assistance, I am convinced, should not be on a piecemeal basis as various crises develop.

Any assistance that this Government may render in the future should be a cure rather than a mere palliative. Any government that is willing to assist in the task of recovery will find full co-operation, I am sure, on the part of the United States Government. Any government which maneuvers to block the recovery of other countries cannot expect help from us. Furthermore, governments, political parties or groups which seek to perpetuate human misery in order to profit therefrom politically or otherwise will encounter the opposition of the United States...

"It would be neither fitting nor efficacious for our Government to undertake to draw up unilaterally a programme designed to put Europe on its feet economically. This is the business of the Europeans. The initiative, I think, must come from Europe. The role of this country should consist of friendly aid in the drafting of a European programme and of later support for such a programme so far as it may be practical for us to do so. The programme should be a joint one, agreed to by a number, if not all, European nations...

"With foresight and a willingness on the part of our people to face up to the vast responsibilities which history has clearly placed upon our country, the difficulties I have outlined can and will be overcome..."

Reaction from Western Europe, by contrast, was swift and entirely positive. On the day of the speech, Ernest Bevin, the British foreign minister, was informed of its contents by the Washington correspondents of two London dailies, whom Acheson had carefully briefed in advance. That very evening, Bevin called together his closest advisers to frame the British response. "It was like a lifeline to sinking men," he recalled later. "It seemed to bring hope where there was none. The generosity of it was beyond my belief."

On 7 June, Agence France-Presse reported from Paris, in terms plainly inspired by the government. It welcomed "an appeal to the peoples of Europe that will be heard in France with special sympathy because it corresponds to a concern for international organisation and economic recovery that France has always shared". A week later, Georges Bidault, the French foreign minister, invited Bevin to Paris to discuss the plan. On 23 June, just 18 days after the speech, Bevin and Bidault met, again in Paris, with Soviet Foreign Minister Vyacheslav Molotov.

"It seemed to bring hope where there was none"

It was to be a long, contentious and ultimately crucial meeting. Molotov feigned interest in the Marshall proposals, but opposed every French and British idea on how to proceed. With his retinue of 100, Molotov walked out of the meeting under instructions from Moscow. On 3 July, Bidault issued an invitation to all European states (with the provisional exception of fascist Spain) to join a "temporary" organisation to respond to the American offer.

Representatives of 16 countries met in Paris on 12 July, 1947, to form the organisation: Austria, Belgium, Denmark, France, Greece, Iceland, Ireland, Italy, Luxembourg, the Netherlands, Norway, Portugal, Sweden, Switzerland, Turkey and the United Kingdom. It was called the Committee of European Economic Co-operation (CEEC).

Sir Oliver Franks, the British delegate, was named chairman and charged with producing a four-year recovery programme. He completed the task on 12 September.

French Foreign Minister Georges Bidault signs OEEC Charter, 16 April, 1948

British Foreign Minister Ernest Bevin, July, 1947

During the July conference, Bevin had stressed that "we have no idea of setting up a permanent organisation to rival the United Nations; it is a piece of *ad hoc* machinery to grapple with a single task". Sir Oliver's report in September echoed the same views. But the Americans saw the matter differently. They felt that the Marshall Plan could only succeed if it fostered permanent co-operation among the European states. Throughout the spring of 1948, Under-Secretary Clayton and his associates lobbied European governments to negotiate and establish a substantial body to deal with the US Economic Co-operation Agency (ECA). With considerable reluctance, the sixteen acceded to Washington's request.

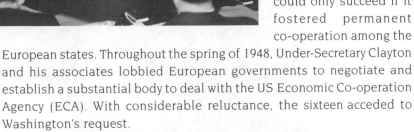

From left: Soviet Foreign Minister Molotov, former US Secretary of State James Byrnes, British Foreign Minister Bevin, French Foreign Minister Bidault. Paris, at the Paris Conference, 1947

On 16 April, 1948, they created an organisation unique in European history, the Organisation for European Economic Co-operation. Named to head it was Robert Marjolin, a 37-year-old French economist with an American wife. (Marjolin stepped down in 1954, to be replaced by René Sergent, another top French civil servant, who served till 1960.)

OEEC was to live and flourish for 13 years; in 1961, it would give birth to the Organisation for Economic Co-operation and Development, including the United States and Canada along with the European nations. It would, under its two names, pilot a half-century of unexampled co-operation, first among Europeans, then among industrial democracies around the world.

Arrivals and coverage of signing of OEEC Charter, April 1946

OECD MEMBER COUNTRIES

OEEC *members*

Austria
Belgium
Denmark
France
Germany
Greece
Iceland
Ireland
Italy
Luxembourg
The Netherlands
Norway
Portugal
Spain
Sweden
Switzerland
Turkey
United Kingdom

OECD *members*
(as well as OEEC countries):

Canada (founding member)
United States (founding member)
Japan (1964)
Finland (1969)
Australia (1971)
New Zealand (1973)
Mexico (1994)
Czech Republic (1995)
Hungary (1996)
Poland (1996)
Korea (1996)

The Marshall Plan was already running full-throttle. The Americans had set up ECA headquarters in the stately Hôtel Talleyrand just off the Place de la Concorde. Paul Hoffman, the internationally-minded and very successful president of the Studebaker Corporation, was named to head it (after Acheson declined). Averell Harriman, the millionaire diplomat who would go on to be ambassador to the Soviet Union and governor of New York, was named as ECA's special representative in Europe. Some 400 Americans, from inside and outside government, staffed the new programme.

By all accounts, the first two or three years of the plan's operations were heady times. European officials rushed in and out of the Talleyrand building, each intent on a project more urgent than all others. Telephones rang off the hook, teleprinters jangled. The experts and dreamers gathered evenings in the bar of the nearby Hôtel Crillon and, over dry martinis, discussed how to move millions of tons of wheat from one continent to another. With Hoffman and Harriman, Marjolin made up the script as they went along. Their primary concern was to cut red tape, to keep the aid moving.

Paul Hoffman

Averell Harriman

BUILDING PASS

ECONOMIC COOPERATION ADMINISTRATION

OFFICE OF THE SPECIAL REPRESENTATIVE

PARIS

No. 1680   EXPIRATION DATE

TO AUTHORIZE
ECA.

PRESENTATION

2. THIS PASS SHOULD
   UPON REQUEST.

3. WHEN THE HOLDER IS TRANSFERRED FROM PARIS THE
   PASS SHOULD BE RETURNED TO ECA PERSONNEL
   SECTION.

4. LOSS OF PASS SHOULD BE REPORTED IMMEDIATELY TO
   ECA PERSONNEL SECTION.

MARIE-ANNE DE SPETH
ISSUED TO

HEIGHT   1m68
WEIGHT   51 Kls
EYES   Brown
SEX   F

SIGNATURE OF HOLDER   ISSUING OFFICER

A recent book by Jacob Kaplan and Gunther Schleiminger, *The European Payments Union: Financial Diplomacy in the 1950s*, describes the key officials of the period as "products of an era of unparalleled destruction" who "were impelled to create, construct and concur. Theirs was an age that relished and nourished interdependence, and they were its ready and able servants."

Liberty ships and commandeered ocean liners already plied the Atlantic, carrying mostly food at first, then – increasingly over the next four years – fuel, fertiliser, raw materials and semi-finished products. Closed and shuttered factories from Lisbon to Oslo chugged back to life. Trade among the Europeans shot ahead; by the end of 1959, it had reached pre-war levels. In the end, direct Marshall Plan aid would reach $13 billion and transform the face of Europe.

But there were overwhelming problems along the way.

Secretary-General
Robert Marjolin
on first anniversary
of OEEC,
16 April, 1949

In 1948, the American Congress voted $500 million less in Marshall aid than the Europeans had requested. Harriman told Marjolin that it would be up to his organisation to allot the shortfalls. The OEEC Council howled; the task seemed impossible. Eventually, though, Europe had no choice. Marjolin sliced the Gordian knot by naming a "restricted committee" of four senior civil servants – from Britain, France, Italy and the Netherlands. The experts heard arguments from each national delegation, then retired to the pleasant village of Chantilly, north of Paris, to write their report in peace. When they presented it to the Council, a violent shouting match took place. Some of the committee's proposals were amended, but finally the experts' overall plan was adopted. The restricted committee device would be used again the following year, when an even sharper cut in funds produced an even tenser situation in the OEEC.

Richard Mayne, a historian of the era, remarks dryly: "Necessity in the face of Congress had been the mother of the OEEC's invention."

WIR BAUEN

EIN NEUES EUROPA

ERP

Fifth place winner in OEEC poster competition, 1950, by Kurt Krepeik, Vienna, Austria

Just as much innovative thinking was required to deal with what economists believed was Europe's deepest structural problem, the paralysis of intra-European trade. Ever since the Great Depression of the 1930s, nationalistic governments had sought to "protect" their home industries from foreign competition by imposing import quotas on various products. Each such move provoked a reprisal from the affected government. Eventually, a web of trade restrictions was woven which clogged commerce throughout the region and stifled, rather than protected, industrial development.

After long debate, OEEC members agreed on 2 November, 1949 to reduce quantitative restrictions on at least 50 per cent of their total trade by 15 December of the same year. Ten of the sixteen kept their promise. Then, on 18 August, 1950, the Organisation adopted a Code of Liberalisation. Quotas and other restrictions fell regularly till 1955, when OEEC countries adopted a goal of 90 per cent trade free of import quotas. In 1961, when the OEEC transformed itself into the OECD, only 5 per cent of European trade, mainly in agriculture, was still subject to quotas.

But trade could not flourish unless the trading partners could pay what they owed each other. Lacking an efficient clearing house for international payments, European governments hoarded gold and dollars. Two-thirds of intra-European trade in the immediate postwar period was conducted through bilateral payments agreements that were really a sophisticated form of barter. A first stab at creating a multilateral payments system came in late 1947,

when Italy and the Benelux countries adopted an agreement of Multilateral Monetary Compensation – a step in the right direction, but a small step indeed.

In 1949, Washington declared that Marshall Plan aid would be "conditional" on the recipients' granting equivalent sums, to be known as "drawing rights," to their European debtors. Finally, on 7 July, 1950, OEEC created a real clearance system, the European Payments Union (EPU). It was announced and explained in a press release that became a classic of the genre:

> "If four people play bridge during an evening, they may settle their debts at the end of each rubber. But if they change partners continually, they may prefer to keep the score on a piece of paper and only settle at the end of the evening. Only the players who are net losers will pay; only the net winners will receive."

A year after its inception, EPU's score-sheet showed transactions of $250 million a month. Working through the Bank for International Settlements in Basel, the Union offered OEEC countries a convenience and flexibility in currency transactions that they had never known. In its absence, the explosion of intra-European trade in the 1950s would never have happened. Its final success was to make itself unnecessary; in 1958, OEEC currencies became convertible among themselves.

Signing ceremony, European Payments Union, September 1950. From left: US Special Representative Milton Katz, Chair of OECD Council Herbert Prack of Austria, Robert Marjolin

An economic boom. Unprecedented growth in trade. A European Payments Union that worked. Three notable successes.

But the fourth major goal of the new organisation proved impossible to realise: a European customs union that would develop into a true common market. A number of European leaders saw such an institution as a vital goal. "To the dogma of national independence," said Count Carlo Sforza, the Italian foreign minister in 1947, "we must add the dogma of European independence". Washington backed the customs union idea to the hilt. At American urging, OEEC created a number of committees to study the issue.

But the political will to accept the limits on national sovereignty simply did not exist in some countries. The United Kingdom, still concentrating on the Commonwealth and its "special relationship" with the United States, opposed closer integration with the Continent. (Indeed, Britain in the 1940s acted successfully to limit the scope and power of the OEEC itself.)

On the other hand, the founders of the European Coal and Steel Community (France, Italy, West Germany and the Benelux countries) decided to go ahead and create not only a true customs union, but also the basis for further integration – what would become the European Economic Community, now the European Union.

The idea of an OEEC customs union was shelved – only to be revived again in 1957, in the form of a British-backed proposal for a European Free Trade Area. This time, it was France that opposed the initiative. Europe, in effect, separated into two distinct trading areas: the European Economic Community; and the European Free Trade Area, EFTA, with Britain, Scandinavia, Portugal, neutral Switzerland and Austria.

Failure to create a Europe-wide customs union deeply disappointed European integrationists, but it took nothing away from the extraordinary achievements of the Marshall Plan and the early OEEC.

Robert Schuman (centre-left); Konrad Adenauer (centre-right); April, 1951

Five years after the start of the plan, its success was dramatic and undeniable. France's harbours, two-thirds of them destroyed in the war, had been entirely rebuilt, and the French ended food rationing in 1949. Italy, though politically fragile, had embarked on a course of industrial development that would lead it to the top of the world's prosperity tables. Nowhere were the fruits of international co-operation sweeter than in Western Germany. There, steel production doubled and quadrupled; trade rose twice, thrice, ten times. By 1953, the Germans were producing twice as many cars as they had made in 1936.

The $13 billion that the United States had spent in Marshall aid combined with Europe's newfound co-operation operated, as Lord Maynard Keynes had predicted: with a powerful "multiplier effect". Recovery spurred recovery. Business sired business. Prosperity produced a high degree of political stability as the Communist threat in France and Italy receded.

"What made the Marshall Plan epoch-making is not only its generosity, but also its philosophy"

With American help, the OEEC had produced what one of its early members called "the strongest argument for free enterprise, democracy and international co-operation the world has ever seen".

Thorkil Kristensen, who was to become the first Secretary-General of the OECD, put it this way: "What made the Marshall Plan epoch-making is not only its generosity, but also its philosophy. *It was a Plan.*"

Rebuilding European industries

Chapter III

Crisis Management

or

History Won't Sit Still

Crisis management
or History Won't Sit Still

AT LEAST in retrospect, the years from 1947 to 1973 appear as the glory days of the OEEC and OECD – the *"trente glorieuses"* as the French still call them, with allowable Gallic hyperbole. They were years of constant, sustained growth in both Europe and North America. Productivity rose steadily in all the industrialised democracies. Consumption, public and private, galloped ahead at an unprecedented 5 per cent a year. Unemployment and inflation both remained in check. Europe's booming economies provided surpluses which they used to endow the generous social programmes that became known as the Welfare State.

But growth was not quite symmetrical. While the United States remained the dominant economic and military power, the OEEC countries rapidly increased their share of the world's wealth and trade. By the late 1950s, Western Europe had shaken off the appearance of a poor, crippled cousin. It had become a near-equal of the US economically, a robust partner and a potent competitor to be reckoned with. Japan, too, had emerged from its postwar morass and was on the brink of becoming a major player on the world stage. The OEEC set-up, with Europe inside and America playing the role of outside benefactor, no longer corresponded to the realities of an increasingly multi-polar world.

Moreover, the break-up of European empires in Africa and the Far East had added a host of new and unpredictable actors to the world scene. Most of these new countries desperately required aid and guidance and looked to the Western democracies to provide it. (And in those Cold War days, if aid from the West was not forthcoming, the potential beneficiaries could always turn to the Soviet Union.)

But not everyone agreed on how to respond. One group of countries, led by Britain, felt the OEEC should be kept as-was; France, Germany and the United States thought a new world environment called for a whole new organisation. In 1959, US President Dwight D. Eisenhower, Chancellor Konrad Adenauer of Germany and President Charles de Gaulle of France put forward a proposal to reform the OEEC.

They felt that the balance of economic power among the developed nations and the urgent demands of the Third World warranted a major and dramatic shift in the institutional arrangements of the West. On 30 September, 1961, the OEEC went out of existence and was replaced by the OECD, including all the members of the original organisation plus the United States and Canada. Japan joined three years later.

Signature
of OECD
Convention,
14 December,
1960

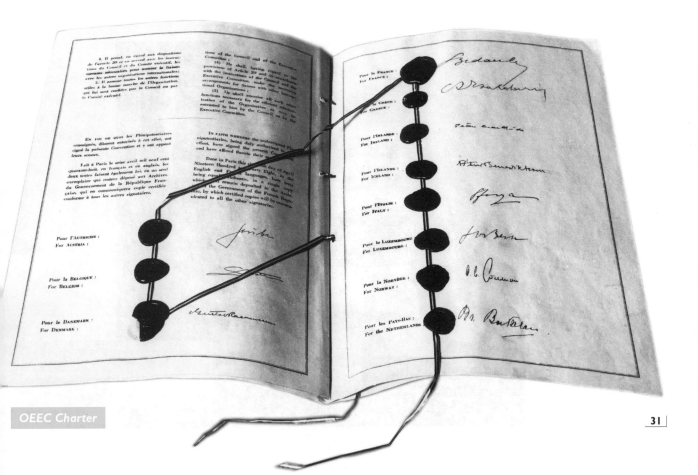

OEEC Charter

Not much changed, and everything changed.

Thorkil Kristensen of Denmark, named Secretary-General of OEEC a year earlier, remained as head of the new Organisation, sitting at the same desk in the stately Château de la Muette. The OECD professed the same principles as its predecessor and shared the same goals. All members recognised the founding principle of the OEEC: that "their economic systems are interrelated and that the prosperity of each of them depends on the prosperity of all". They expressed their commitment to free trade and their obligation to aid the poorer nations to develop their economies.

From the earliest days after the Organisation's name change and expansion, its chief concern was with macroeconomic policy co-ordination. The Economic Policy Committee stood at its centre, with its celebrated Working Parties, especially Working Party No. 3, on Better International Payments Equilibrium. More prosaically, but just as importantly, the new OECD continued OEEC's pioneering efforts to provide timely, accurate and reliable statistics on member-state economies. Indeed, one of the Organisation's most original and important accomplishments has been the evolution of an increasingly sophisticated approach to national accounting techniques. The economic and policy analysis that go hand-in-hand with reliable comparative statistics have made the OECD's semi-annual *Economic Outlook* and its annual country studies authoritative reference works worldwide. Many distinguished statisticians and economists contributed to OECD work, but the guiding spirit on the statistical side was Richard Stone, a Cambridge professor, who received the Nobel prize in economics in 1984.

Former US President John Kennedy with first OECD Secretary-General Thorkil Kristensen, 1961

Both the old and the new Organisation worked extensively on agricultural and fisheries issues, monitoring and encouraging a green revolution in Western Europe that converted the region from a heavy net importer of food to one of the world's leading exporters. OECD also continued OEEC's function as a promoter of industry and a conduit for the exchange of technological work. The trail-blazing work of the European Productivity Agency, created in 1953, was taken over by a Directorate for Industry, which has since been expanded to include science and technology as well.

Continuity, then, but also deep change.

With the US, Canada and Japan, and, later, Australia, New Zealand and Finland, the Organisation more than doubled its economic gravity. It now produced more than two-thirds of the world's goods, and accounted for more than four-fifths of its trade. In purely economic terms, it represented a greater proportion of world wealth and productive capacity in one co-ordinated economic body than had ever been seen, or is likely to be seen again. On the political side, it stood as a colossal, and colossally successful, challenge to Soviet and Chinese Communism.

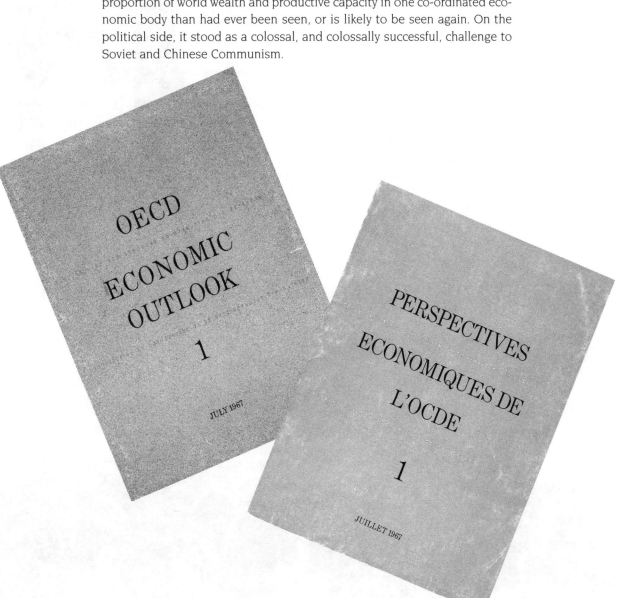

OECD ECONOMIC OUTLOOK

1

JULY 1967

PERSPECTIVES ECONOMIQUES DE L'OCDE

1

JUILLET 1967

All the old-timers agree: the atmosphere of OECD in the 1960s and early 1970s was electric with enthusiasm, heady with a sense of universal responsibility.

Nowhere was that mix more intoxicating than in the bi-monthly meetings of WP-3, where national officials and OECD experts felt themselves to be standing at the helm of the world's leading economies. This group was first chaired by Emile van Lennep, who later served as the Secretary-General; it soon became the Organisation's most famous and influential body. Composed of senior treasury officials and advised by OECD's most distinguished economists, it monitored and helped shape member countries' macroeconomic policies throughout the 1960s and well into the 1970s. For its advocates, WP-3 played a heroic role in "fine-tuning" Western economies during their years of galloping growth. Its critics paid it unintentional honour by describing it as the inner sanctum of a rich-country conspiracy to rule the world.

In the early days, most of its members marched to the music of Lord Maynard Keynes, the eminent economic theorist who had advised both Franklin Roosevelt and Winston Churchill. With Keynes, they believed that prosperity and full employment could be maintained almost indefinitely if overall demand were deftly controlled within a given system.

One senior OECD economist of the period recalls: "The first proposition was that the major countries were collectively responsible for maintaining the right level of demand in the world economy. They would have to meet together and form a consensus as to whether the dangers in the world were those of inflation or deflation; if the world looked too inflationary, then it was the countries with the highest rates of inflation and the fastest rates of growth which should take restrictive action; if it looked deflationary, it was the countries

Sir Hugh Ellis-Rees, first Chair of Economic Policy Committee

Meeting of WP-3, October 1971.
Dr. Otmar Emminger of Germany ("President");
to right: John Dow, Assistant Secretary-General;
John Fay, Director Economics and Statistics;
Gerald Eldin, Deputy Secretary-General

with the lowest rates of inflation and the highest rate of unemployment who should take expansionary action."

Sounds simple? It didn't always seem so at the time. Arguments raged inside WP-3, between the pure Keynesians and those who placed the emphasis on balanced budgets and minimal inflation. The 1959 recession in the United States pitted American officials against the Germans. Washington demanded that Bonn take strong expansionary measures and thereby act as a "loco-motive" for the other OECD economies. The Germans, haunted by memo-ries of runaway inflation in the years between the two world wars, refused to budge from their conservative fiscal stance. The same issue flamed up in 1966 and 1967, with much the same arguments, although this time the Germans did agree to take stimulative measures.

On the whole, though, Keynes's elegant model worked almost magically in the economic environment of the 1960s. Stable exchange rates, based on the dollar's convertibility into gold, underpinned growth and trade. Cheap and abundant energy, especially Middle Eastern oil, fueled the ongoing industrial boom. Technological innovation in chemistry and medi-cine, agriculture and computers, smoothed the massive displacement of populations from farm to city, from factory to services. Intimate co-operation among the economically dominant OECD countries headed off one looming crisis after another.

To many, the OECD goal of "sustainable economic growth" seemed not only achievable, but actually in place.

Krupp factory,
Germany

There were, however, several worms in the apple.

A first warning signal came in the late 1960s, when a wave of student demonstrations began in the United States, then spread across Western Europe, culminating in the colourful chaos of Paris's "May '68". At the same time, discontented European workers staged one strike after another, demanding a larger share of the economic pie. Clearly, the comfortable consumer society that OECD members had built on the ruins of World War II had failed to satisfy the psychological demands of many who benefited from it.

Nor was the system itself quite so invulnerable as it appeared. While economies in North America and Western Europe continued to grow steadily, the United Kingdom lagged behind the others. At least one major reason was an overvalued pound sterling, a major reserve currency. Successive British governments resisted a devaluation, mainly on political grounds. In 1967, the United Kingdom was finally forced to devalue. That left the dollar as the world's only true reserve currency. But the dollar had its problems as well. Sound though the US economy undoubtedly was, it went into recession in 1970, partly as a result of economic dislocations due to the Vietnam war. The American trade surplus diminished. On 15 August, 1971, President Richard Nixon announced that the dollar would no longer be convertible into gold.

Former US President Richard Nixon

Paris, 1968 (below); Netherlands, 1973 (opposite)

With a single sentence, Nixon kicked the principal prop out from under the international monetary arrangements that had prevailed since World War II. The Bretton Woods agreement, based on the dollar's strength, became a dead letter. No longer pegged to gold, the US currency "floated," as did all others. The values of the Deutschemark and the yen shot up. No one knew what was likely to happen next. The OECD view was that its member nations could control the situation by negotiating a new set of exchange rates that reflected actual conditions in world markets – and making them stick. The so-called Group of Ten nations, consisting of the largest Western economies, gathered in December 1971 at the Smithsonian Institution in Washington with experts from OECD and the IMF. They hammered out the new rates, and the rates more or less held – at least for the first year.

The sense of crisis diminished. But worse, much worse, was on the way. Suddenly, the Keynesian economic model seemed no longer to fit the facts. Inflation in the OECD area rose over 8 per cent in 1972-1973, and despite robust economic growth, unemployment spiked up, for the first time since 1947. As far back as the late '60s the OECD had begun warning of a coming burst in inflation, and in January, 1973, several experts in the Economics Department suggested that a substantial increase in the price of oil – from about $2 a barrel to $5 – might occur and would have unpredictable consequences.

Former US Secretary of State Henry Kissinger

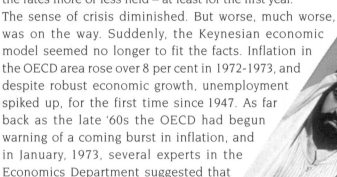

Few people, even inside the Organisation, listened seriously to the warning at the time; they were much too worried about the imminent breakdown of the Smithsonian agreement, which fell apart two months later. But a special group of middle-level OECD officials continued modelling the possible outcomes of a sudden rise in oil prices. They completed their study at the end of September, 1973, just days before the outbreak of the Yom Kippur war.

This time, the OECD and its members faced what was obviously a worldwide crisis of enormous proportions. And the Organisation earned its spurs as a crisis manager.

By December, the Organisation of Petroleum Exporting Companies had quadrupled the price of crude oil to $9. It halted all shipments to the US, Denmark, the Netherlands and Portugal. The embargo hit the Dutch worst, virtually eliminating automobile traffic and, overnight, creating a nation of bicyclists. Else-

where in Europe and the United States, motorists lined up by the hundreds at gas stations that often had no fuel to offer. French President Valéry Giscard-d'Estaing reduced the temperature at the Élysée Palace to 20 degrees centigrade, had himself photographed in a cardigan sweater and urged his countrymen to follow his example. Soon energy-saving rules and legislation came into force throughout the Western world.

So much for the folklore. OECD economists, meanwhile, were at work predicting the true consequences of the crisis: a rise in inflation from 9 per cent to the mid-teens; a traumatic drop in demand that would translate into a 6 per cent slump in OECD-country growth rates.

First IEA Executive Director Ulf Lantzke (front) and Chairman of IEA Board, Étienne Davignon, 1975

Israel, 1973. Yom Kippur War

There was, however, a potential silver lining to the cloud. The vast increase in the wealth of OPEC countries would have to be invested somewhere. And where else but in the economies of the advanced industrialised states? The idea of "recycling petro-dollars" was born.

There followed a series of cloak-and-dagger meetings between OECD figures and Sheik Ahmed Zaki Yamani, the flamboyant Saudi energy minister. The point of the secret meetings was to persuade OPEC leaders of the wisdom of the recycling idea. They were arranged by a young television journalist, Christine Ockrent, whose father, Roger Ockrent, was then Belgian Ambassador to OECD. (Christine had met Yamani while reporting in the Middle East.) In luxury hotels in Zurich, Rome and Vienna, envoys from Paris met with OPEC leaders and sought to convince them both of the suicidal madness of further price increases and the virtues of recycling their new riches.

That was OECD's backstage response. The public reaction was dramatic, unusual and successful. On 12 December, 1973, Henry Kissinger, the American secretary of state, declared in a speech in London that the oil crisis could be "the economic equivalent of the sputnik challenge of 1957". The West, Kissinger argued, should use the present calamity to correct its oil-supply weaknesses, and correct them fast. He suggested the creation of an "Energy Action Group" to counter OPEC's power, to ensure reliable oil supplies to the Western democracies and to deal with the catastrophic economic and social consequences of the energy price rise.

Sheik Ahmed Zaki Yamani following OPEC meeting, 1983

On 10 February, 1974, ministers from 13 major consuming countries – all OECD members – met in Washington and created an "Energy Co-ordinating Group". The group's task: to develop policies for energy conservation, demand restraint, emergency allocation of oil supplies and the accelerated development of alternative energy sources. Ockrent was named to head the group, but he died a few weeks later and was replaced by his fellow-Belgian, Étienne Davignon. Ockrent's contribution to the OECD was honoured by the Organisation when it named the Château's most ornate meeting room after him.

By November of 1974, Davignon and his colleagues had decided that their group should take a more formal shape, as the International Energy Agency, "within the framework of OECD" but with a separate governing board and a degree of autonomy. That autonomy was needed for two main reasons. First, the IEA would have to implement a precise and detailed energy policy, involving the systematic build-up of emergency stocks in member countries and their allocation in times of crisis – not the kind of job the OECD was set up to do. Second, the French government did not wish to join, so that IEA and OECD membership would not be identical. (France, in fact, objected to the US initiative and there was some doubt that the OECD framework could be used if France vetoed the creation of the energy agency. In the end, France abstained and the IEA formed part of the OECD. France finally joined the IEA in 1994.)

Saint-Laurent-des-Eaux
Nuclear Plant, France

Under the leadership of Ulf Lantzke of Germany, the IEA's first Executive Director, member countries pledged to cut their oil imports by 2 million barrels a day in 1975. They also agreed to increase stocks available for an emergency to 70 days of oil imports by the beginning of 1976. The undertaking was increased to 90 days by 1980. Intensive research was launched on coal technology and on alternative energy sources.

Much in the same way as NATO, the IEA won its war without ever having to fight it. The combination of decreased oil imports, improved emergency stocks and an elaborate sharing system for times of crisis discouraged OPEC from mounting another embargo. In 1979, when oil prices spiked up for a second time, and during the Gulf War in 1991, the mere existence of a convincing Western defence sufficed to parry the potential threat. The oil-sharing agreement has never had to be put into effect.

On the economic side, the oil shock was but the beginning of a decade of difficulty. First a deep recession, then a combination of low growth and rapidly rising prices – "stagflation" – further weakened the "Keynesian consensus" that had been OECD gospel. More and more, the Organisation's economists concentrated on monetary issues rather than the fiscal "fine-tuning" of the 1960s. Inflation came to be seen as the primary villain in economic life, to be battered with every possible policy instrument. The experts began to look critically at the huge increases in public-sector employment and welfare programmes – and to question their sustainability. The second oil shock in 1979 shifted the OECD's Economics Department further to the supply-side approaches associated with the University of Chicago.

So moved the world. President Ronald Reagan and Prime Minister Margaret Thatcher launched programmes of structural adjustment that precisely reflected the new school of OECD thinking. Seen from a distance of almost 20 years, the 1970s were a period of almost constant upheaval and difficulty. And yet, the economic threats were all contained. The Organisation's member countries entered the 1980s much altered but still very prosperous. None of the really disastrous scenarios – except for high and persistent unemployment in Europe – came true. The OECD had managed a major crisis, and succeeded.

The shocks of 1973 and 1979 signaled even deeper changes in the relative positions of nations across the economic checkerboard. While steady progress interrupted by occasional recessions and steadily rising unemployment continued in OECD countries, the rest of the world changed radically and often with dismaying speed. After the oil-rich Middle Eastern countries, the vibrant "tigers" of South-East Asia achieved startling and sustained growth. The OECD responded forthrightly by beginning a programme of regular dialogue with the dynamic Asian economies. In Latin America, some countries bounded ahead while others foundered in debt, and runaway inflation affected all. Sub-Saharan Africa and much of the Indian sub-continent grew relatively poorer by the year, while India itself achieved food self-sufficiency despite a relentlessly rising population. Most of the thinking about development assistance that prevailed when the OEEC became the OECD proved wrong, some of it deeply pernicious. The very notion of a "Third World" foundered as some of its members grew rapidly rich while others were mired in poverty, corruption and even tragic bouts of starvation.

Former UK Minister for Overseas Development Baroness Chalker

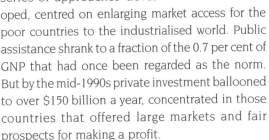

Inside the OECD, the Development Assistance Committee and the Trade Directorate became focal points of the West's efforts to deal with an external environment that seemed to defy all logic. Over the decades, a whole new series of approaches developed, centred on enlarging market access for the poor countries to the industrialised world. Public assistance shrank to a fraction of the 0.7 per cent of GNP that had once been regarded as the norm. But by the mid-1990s private investment ballooned to over $150 billion a year, concentrated in those countries that offered large markets and fair prospects for making a profit.

New strategies for public aid and investment, most of them fostered by the DAC, concentrated on supporting indigenous investment and entrepreneurship. Technical expertise and training, rather than big chunks of money, were increasingly seen as the best route out of national poverty.

Today, OECD differentiates among half-a-dozen kinds of relations with "Third World" nations, some in groupings of "dynamic countries", some as "dialogue partners", some as "newly industrialising". The scatter-shot assault on world poverty of the 1960s has given way to an extremely sophisticated and flexible set of links with partners across the world.

Though quieter and more evolutionary than the theatrics of the oil crises, the shift in OECD's way of relating to its partners and neighbours has been no less significant and crucial for the future.

A very different challenge erupted in the late autumn of 1989. To the astonishment of nearly everyone, the apparently monolithic Soviet empire in Eastern Europe began to crumble. Hungary and Czechoslovakia shook off Communist rule. The Berlin Wall opened and the 17 million people of East Germany were suddenly free. Romanians staged a short but bloody revolution and executed their dictators. More quietly, Bulgaria sloughed off Soviet rule.

Wonderful news? It certainly was. A hundred million people were suddenly free of totalitarian rule and of a dysfunctional economy. A shining dream had come true.

But the morning after brought a thousand headaches. Not only did the new democracies have to create a brand-new set of political institutions, they had to re-create free economies out of the rubble of state central planning. They lacked even the most rudimentary tools: a banking system, reliable statistics, management techniques. In the wake of their velvet revolutions, production plunged, the old distribution systems collapsed, runaway inflation pauperised whole sections of the population, especially old people living on fixed pensions.

The first months of 1990 saw a free-ranging debate within OECD, as in every member country capital. What, to use Lenin's phrase, was to be done? In Paris, Jean-Claude Paye, the French OECD Secretary-General, proposed an ambitious programme based on the Organisation's existing strengths. What OECD could bring to the former Soviet satellites – dubbed Economies in Transition – was a wealth of expertise, analytical skill and policy know-how.

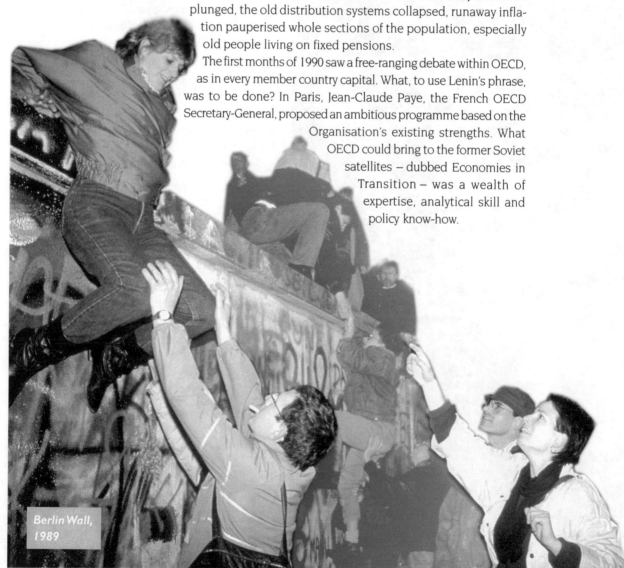

Berlin Wall, 1989

Within months, a centre to co-ordinate work with the new market economies had been set up. Experts from Paris, often with teams of experts from member countries, fanned out across the region, offering advice on everything from modern tax collection techniques to how to organise a responsible civil service. What was later called the Centre for Co-operation with the Economies in Transition, CCET, sponsored scores of seminars and training sessions for officials and entrepreneurs from the transition countries

Specific programmes were geared to individual countries and groups of countries. In 1991, the most advanced group – Poland, Hungary and Czechoslovakia – became Partners in Transition, a programme to help them prepare for OECD membership. The first two and the Czech Republic had already become full members of OECD by 1996, with Slovakia heading for membership. Separate programmes were tailored for the Balkan states and the Russian Federation. In 1996, Russia, which had signed a declaration of co-operation in 1994, formally asked to join.

OECD prepared country studies of the transition countries, beginning with Hungary. Drawing on the resources of half a dozen different directorates, the Organisation offered advice on tax policy, trade policy reform, competition, unemployment and social issues, education and industrial restructuring. A key element in the programme is SIGMA – Support for Improvement in Governance and Management in Central and Eastern European Countries – run jointly by OECD and the European Union. Sigma holds seminars and offers hands-on advice on such basic issues as statistics, public procurement, the policy-making process and administrative oversight.

Moscow

The task is by no means complete. The former Communist economies have not responded to outside aid and stimulation as did Western Europe to the Marshall Plan. But progress is evident. Privatisation has proceeded in many countries at a rapid pace. Runaway inflation has been contained. Banks have sprouted up and entrepreneurs have emerged. It may be decades before some of the most remote of the former Soviet republics approach Western levels of production and stability. But the ground has been broken.

OECD – in partnership with member countries and other international organisations – has met its second major crisis and is handling it.

Secretary-General Donald Johnston with Romanian President Emil Constantinescu (upper); Polish Deputy Prime Minister Grzegorz Kolodko (lower)

Chapter IV

Coming of Age: the van Lennep and Paye Eras

Coming of Age:
the van Lennep and Paye Eras

CRISES filled the headlines and occupied a lot of OECD attention. But crises were far from the whole story. They always are. In the quarter century between 1970 and 1995, an organisation conceived in the shadow of World War II and designed as a short-term, single-task body grew and changed beyond recognition. It shifted its focus from a near-exclusive concentration on macroeconomic issues to a concern with nearly every feature of economic life: trade and taxes, ecology and technology, the Third World and the changing role of women. It abandoned the demand-side economic model proposed by Lord Maynard Keynes and came to champion the supply-side theories evolved at the University of Chicago.

The Organisation honed its methodology, especially in statistics, where it often led the world. It extended its analytical grasp – and its regular reports – to include one new area after another. It came up with formulas for comparing the actual wealth of various countries (not just their per capita GDP), for evaluating the real impact of agricultural subsidies, for apportioning the costs of ecological damage. First governments, then universities, NGOs, journalists and concerned citizens came to rely on OECD analysis and statistics as the most complete and accurate anywhere.

Formed as a purely Western European, then Atlantic, organisation, OECD steadily widened its geographic scope. With the admission of Japan in 1964, then Australia and New Zealand in the early

Emile
van Lennep

1970s, the Organisation extended its influence into the Pacific and Oceania. It also tapped into a deep new pool of talent. While reticent at first to assert themselves in OECD, Japanese officials now fully participate at every level, including to the rank of Deputy Secretary-General and the coveted position of chief economist. By the middle 1990s,

OECD "outreach" extended in all directions: to the booming economies of South-East Asia, to the former Soviet Union and its former satellites, to China and India, to Latin America; it continued its work of monitoring aid to Africa and other developing countries. In a globalising world, OECD had become a global organisation.

And it has evolved a style. Independent, it criticises less-than-best practice in members and non-members alike. (The German government once issued an instant and furious press release to refute OECD arguments in a just-published report. Other countries have held up publication of their Economic Surveys for months trying to persuade their peers of a different tone or prescription – only sometimes successfully). It treasures discretion, although it occasionally serves as a stage for vociferous and even pungent public debate; witness the news-conference battles at the OECD between Mickey Kantor and Sir Leon Brittan, the American and European negotiators in the Uruguay Round of trade talks that concluded in 1993. Global in its concerns, it gets into the nitty-gritty of microeconomic behaviour. It follows the new world maxim, "Think global, but act local".

Jean-Claude Paye

OECD's apparent paradoxes and constantly evolving priorities have baffled many an observer and generated some unflattering sobriquets in the press: "the rich countries' club", "the talking-shop", "the high-price think-tank". In fact, there is some truth in each of those tags. But they fail to capture the uniqueness of the place: its consistent ability to blend academic theory and real-time analysis, to produce policy advice that responds to the member countries' needs.

Hundreds of OECD people have contributed significantly to its ongoing evolution. But two men held the tiller through more than half the Organisation's life: Emile van Lennep, Secretary-General from 1969 to 1984; and Jean-Claude Paye, who succeeded him, serving until 1996. Each left an indelible mark.

They could scarcely have been more unalike, at least on the surface. Van Lennep, a bull-necked Dutch lawyer and a passionate Keynesian, loved the rough-and-tumble of political dispute, was a superb lobbyist and champion of his staff's ideas. Paye, an elegant product of France's elite public service and an economic pragmatist, shunned centre stage and concentrated on improving and extending the Organisation's analytic capacities. Yet, despite their very marked differences in style and character, each man participated in what, with hindsight at least, appears a nearly seamless process of change and adaptation. Indeed, some initiatives which would appear typical of one man's thinking were taken by the other.

Gro Harlem Brundtland of Norway, Chair of first OECD Environment ministerial

Van Lennep's stewardship began in the heyday of Keynesianism; one of OECD's nicknames at the time was "the house that Keynes built". The new Secretary-General had already chaired the Organisation's Economic Policy Committee and its Working Party No. 3. He was, rightly, considered a leading exponent of the dominant economic thinking, a fine-tuner to his fingertips. He was to change his views progressively through the 1970s, but he remained convinced that economic policy would be, and should be, the central business of the Organisation. He participated actively in the stormy debates of the 1970s, publicly urging Germany to reflate and act as the locomotive for European recovery, chastising the administration in Washington for running extravagant trade and budget deficits.

But van Lennep's contribution scarcely stopped there. On his retirement in 1984, he described his most satisfying achievement at OECD as the Trade Pledge of 1974. That document, adopted by all the Organisation's members, was aimed at heading off what van Lennep saw as a dangerous rush toward protectionism in the wake of the first oil crisis. In it, the signatories agreed to impose no new tariffs or quotas on one another's exports. It succeeded in averting a possible trade war, and it became the basis for the "standstill and rollback" strategy later employed in the Tokyo Round of trade talks under the General Agreement on Tariffs and Trade.

One of van Lennep's first major decisions was to create a full-scale directorate on environmental policy in 1970. OECD was the first international organisation to take such a step, and it has remained a leader in the field ever since.

Between 1972 and 1974, the new directorate adopted what has become known as the "polluter pays" principle, which has become a cornerstone of environmental policy within and outside OECD. Simply put, it requires those who pollute the environment not only to pay for the damage they inflict, even accidentally, but also to bear the costs of pollution prevention and control measures. Affected industries fought hard to head off the principle, and many countries sought exceptions to the general rule, but it was unanimously adopted, most exceptions were ultimately dropped and it now serves as a universal standard.

Beyond the formulation of the "polluter pays" principle and the enforcement review it entails, the Directorate has branched out to cover virtually every aspect of environmental protection, from acid rain in Germany to automobile emissions in Japan. It is heavily involved in "horizontal" projects like the interrelation of environmental problems and development aid, how environmental policy can affect trade and how natural resources can be sustained.

WARNING

Fish Contaminated
DO NOT EAT
DO NOT REMOVE SIGN UNDER PENALTY OF LAW
PROPERTY OF MASS. D.E.Q.E.

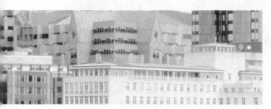

By the time van Lennep took over at the Château, OECD had already built a record as an analyst and idea-spinner in the field of education. The launch of the first Soviet sputnik created a panic in the West and a call for rapid improvements in OECD members' educational systems at all levels. Then as now, the Organisation insisted that members recognise education as an "investment" and judge performance in those terms. With van Lennep's approval, OECD's rigorous reviews of national teaching performance became harder-hitting and more specific, and they still are.

The 1960s had proved beyond possible doubt that the initial notion of "development assistance" to the newly independent colonies of Africa and Asia had been all wet. Tens of billions of dollars in gifts and loans were diverted by corruption, squandered on prestige projects, wasted by economies unprepared to absorb them. One new nation after another stumbled into deep debt, imperilling the Western banking system as a whole.

Emile van Lennep with French President Georges Pompidou, 10th anniversary of OECD, December 1970; Austrian Federal Chancellor Bruno Kreisky; Queen Juliana of the Netherlands

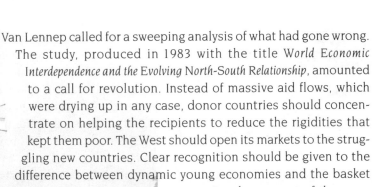

Van Lennep called for a sweeping analysis of what had gone wrong. The study, produced in 1983 with the title *World Economic Interdependence and the Evolving North-South Relationship*, amounted to a call for revolution. Instead of massive aid flows, which were drying up in any case, donor countries should concentrate on helping the recipients to reduce the rigidities that kept them poor. The West should open its markets to the struggling new countries. Clear recognition should be given to the difference between dynamic young economies and the basket cases. For the poorest of the poor, special arrangements like the OECD-sponsored Club du Sahel should be provided. More advanced developers needed completely different treatment. Once again, member countries adopted a view at the OECD that guided their policy for the next 15 years.

James Michel, Chair Development Assistance Committee

One of the oddest functions OECD performed during van Lennep's tenure was as a referee in the violent trans-Atlantic disagreement over technological sales to the Soviet Union. While several European countries proposed to sell sophisticated oil-pipeline equipment to Moscow, the United States argued that the hardware could well be used for military purposes. The squabble should have been settled inside the secretive Cocom organisation (housed in an annexe to the US embassy in Paris), but it spilled onto Page One and seriously threatened to undermine the Western alliance. Van Lennep offered OECD advice and a new venue for the argument, and it was ultimately resolved.

During all this time, of course, the central focus remained on economics: the oil shocks, stagflation, the sudden rise of what looked like enduring – hence structural – unemployment. Throughout the period, van Lennep and his economist colleagues struggled with the issues. Little by little, with frequent reversals and back-sliding, they came to the conclusion that their Keynesian presuppositions were, if not wrong, inappropriate to a new economic environment. Increasingly, their speeches and papers called for "positive adjustment policies," restructuring and fiscal tightening.

The "house that Keynes built" had been converted to a dormitory for supply-siders.

So it was to remain during the 12-year incumbency of Jean-Claude Paye, from 1984 to 1996.

Denounced by conservative "dirigistes" and leftists alike, OECD stuck to its basic message: cut budgets, eliminate labour-market rigidities, free international trade of all remaining barriers, rationalise production and exploit all available new technologies. The call was repeated in one ministerial statement after another. It was reflected in scores of country studies, and adopted as the new orthodoxy by member countries.

It was an easy message to parody and caricature. In France, the OECD was dubbed "the house of the single policy", implying that the Organisation remained insensitive to the pain that restructuring inevitably produces, deaf to the complaints of the jobless, the ageing, those incapable of adapting to a harsh new world.

That was nonsense, of course. Never before in its history had the Organisation been so deeply involved in analysing social issues and producing proposals to limit social damage. It was assumed inside OECD, as in most capitals, that the Welfare State was in crisis and could not survive in the same form as before. There had to be alternatives, but a return to dog-eat-dog Nineteenth-Century capitalism was not one of them. As a Frenchman, a citizen of a state with an elaborate and expensive social protection net, Paye recognised early the imperative need for new thinking, and, from his maiden speech, warned of the adjustments that would be needed to reap the benefits of globalisation.

Some OECD Chief Economists, from left: John Fay, Sylvia Ostry, David Henderson, Kumiharu Shigehara

Part of the effective new thinking he spurred was in the area of trade. OECD was present at the creation of the Uruguay Round of trade negotiations under the GATT. Without the Organisation's contribution, the Round might well have failed. OECD provided encouragement, analysis and numbers to the negotiators – especially in the murky and divisive area of farm subsidies. An OECD study not only calculated the global net savings on subsidies that the terms of the accord would yield at $270 billion a year by 2002. The OECD also calculated Producer Subsidy Equivalents which allowed negotiators to compare such apparent incomparables as state-paid milk for American school-children's lunches and set-aside allowances for European farmers' fallow fields.

Paye also initiated dozens of studies on social issues, most importantly on the effects of an ageing population and on employment in a globalised economic framework (see Chapter VI).

In a universe of explosive and unpredictable technological advance, Paye insisted that OECD keep up with the bewildering new issues that the new technologies raised. (Not even OECD could hope to stay *ahead* of them.) He beefed up the Science and Technology Directorate and set its experts working on exotic issues ranging from cybernetics to bio-technology.

OECD news conference, June 1993, with Mickey Kantor and Sir Leon Brittan (centre left) discussing GATT and trade issues

Paye recalled his dozen years at the OECD as a period in which both the promise and the perils of globalisation became apparent. His own main concern was to try to blunt the impact of rapid structural adjustment on individual citizens. Several member countries refused to listen to his warnings. As a result, the OECD's trailblazing Jobs Study was delayed till 1994; Paye would have liked to see it appear several years earlier.

Now, he feels that the Organisation is on track, but he worries that it is fundamentally "fragile", without funds and without strong bureaucratic support in capitals. He insists that OECD must reach out to the rest of the world, but he is dubious about admitting new members at a rapid pace. For the moment, he recommends that the Organisation serve more and more as a forum for discussions among such regional groups as the European Union, NAFTA and ASEAN.

In fact, it was Paye himself who contributed most to opening the Organisation up to the world around it.

Paradoxically, the bluff and congenial van Lennep had run OECD in quasi-military fashion, discouraging his staff from meeting with the press or even with officials of non-member countries. "You had to fill out a slip," grumbles one old hand, "if you wanted to see a chap from the Brazilian finance ministry." But Paye, personally reserved as he was and trained in the velvety discretion of the French foreign service, opened the doors. He invited journalists in and offered them extensive briefings. He intensified traditional relations with advanced non-member countries.

More: he went seeking new relations, new linkages. Partly at Japanese prompting, he developed a robust dialogue with the Newly Industrial Countries of South-East Asia (NICs, now known as DAEs or Dynamic Asian Economies). He invited them to participate in appropriate studies and discussions in Paris and at workshops on their own turf. One ex-DAE, Korea, is now a member of the Organisation.

Jean-Claude Paye and Chinese Premier Li Peng, Beijing, July 1995

But Paye cast his net still farther. He established dialogue with the industrialising nations of Latin America, especially Brazil, Argentina and Chile. When the Berlin Wall fell, OECD was quick to spin a web of relationships in Central and Eastern Europe, then with the successor states of the Soviet Union. China and India became major partners in dialogue and co-operation. Russia got a special co-operation agreement in 1994 and in 1996 asked to join the OECD.

By the time Paye stepped down, in mid-1996, the wealthy and powerful, but essentially self-regarding, Organisation established in 1948 had become a cosmopolitan centre concerned not merely with economic issues but with virtually every aspect

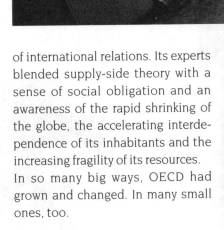

of international relations. Its experts blended supply-side theory with a sense of social obligation and an awareness of the rapid shrinking of the globe, the accelerating interdependence of its inhabitants and the increasing fragility of its resources.

In so many big ways, OECD had grown and changed. In many small ones, too.

New times, new customs.

Some of the changes that have most deeply affected life at OECD may seem quite trivial at first blush. Take coffee. Or cigarettes. As veterans recall it, brainstorming sessions 20 years ago were fuelled with gallons of strong coffee served right at the conference table. "Now what do we get?" one of them asks with disgust. "Mineral water! That's what!" And those heroic meetings took place under a comforting

cloud of blue tobacco smoke. No more, of course. Much of the OECD is a non-smoking area, including conference rooms. The Organisation is more liberal on this point, however, than one might expect; smoking is permitted in parts of all the restaurants and lounges.

Here as elsewhere, health and fitness are in style. There is an OECD hiking club. A jogger can often be glimpsed heading from a Secretariat building to the Bois de Boulogne. Many staff members arrive by bicycle.

New members have brought new accents, even languages. Eavesdrop at a coffee break and enjoy the twang of the Kiwi, the slangy, very un-Castillian Spanish of Mexico. Groups of delegates confer in Czech, gossip in Korean, tell tall tales in Polish. Assimilation has occurred. The Japanese, the first new members after the creation of OECD, spent years baffling their colleagues with their apparent reserve, even passivity. According to old-timers, delegations from Tokyo sat through day-long meetings in utter silence, busily taking notes. That has changed altogether. As Japan has relaxed into the Organisation (and as the quality of Japanese English and French has improved), its representatives have become as voluble as any other participants in this very talkative talk-shop. Aussies and New Zealanders who entered OECD as rowdy beer-drinkers have modulated into suave Parisian wine connoisseurs.

OECD cyclists: Gabriel Drilhon and Alison Benney, 1997

OECD hikers: Miguel Ruiz (centre) with his wife, Janet, and former OECD staffer Mary Dallos (right), 1997

Women at OECD, clockwise from top: Anne Wibble, Sweden, Minister of Finance; Grete Knudsen, Norway, Minister for Trade and Shipping; Senator Jocelyn Newman, Australia, Minister for Social Security; Yvonne van Rooy, Netherlands, Minister for Foreign Trade; Dr Helga Steeg, IEA Executive Director; Tansu Çiller, Turkey, Minister of State for Economic Affairs; Corinne Lepage, France, Environment Minister; Joanna Shelton, USA, OECD Deputy Secretary-General; Vasso Papendreou, Member of the Commission, CEC; Carla Hills, US Trade Representative

But the most radical of all the incremental changes has been the arrival of women – women as government officials, as senior experts, as directors. Observe any photograph of an OEEC or OECD gathering before the early 1970s. What you see is suits, seas of suits, acres of suits, mostly well-tailored, mostly dark and all worn by comfortably paunchy middle-aged men. But no longer. Among the female pioneers were world-class stars like Gro Harlem Brundtland, of Norway. Inside the house, Sylvia Ostry of Canada, chief economist from 1980 to 1983, proved herself not only as competent but every bit as stubborn as any man. Joanna Shelton, an American, holds the No. 2 position in the Secretariat as Deputy Secretary-General, while more and more women serve in posts that were once tacitly reserved to men.

And then, of course, there are the computers. Computers here, there and everywhere, an extremely intricate in-house Intranet network connected to the worldwide Internet. Computers to compile statistics, to dispatch and receive e-mail, to run massive economic models. *Everyone* in the Organisation has a computer, including the building guards, and everyone is expected to operate it at an appropriate level of expertise.

Hence the ubiquity of training courses. Training in cybernetics. Training in languages and management skills. On any given day, dozens of OECDers are to be found in the training rooms on an underground floor of the Franqueville building, sweating over Excel or the Russian language. Not only does the Organisation insist to member countries that continuous adaptation and re-adaptation are the keys to success in the baffling era of globalisation. It practises what it preaches.

THE INNER SANCTUM

Secretive. Ideological. Manipulative. Omnipotent.

Such were the adjectives that economic journalists of the 1960s and 1970s chose to describe OECD's Economic Policy Committee and its celebrated Working Party No. 3. The newspaper image was a caricature, of course, but it contained a grain of truth. As the first and still the most important committee of the "rich countries' club", EPC wielded enormous influence with governments and central banks.

Its views on macroeconomic policy were always listened to and often followed. The still more mysterious WP-3, composed of OECD officials and representatives of the Group of Ten countries – actually eleven: the G-7 plus Sweden, Switzerland, Belgium and the Netherlands – was at least as influential, and even more controversial. Charged with tracking exchange rates, it acted as an informal pilot for macroeconomic policy in all the developed countries.

In a changing world, the roles of both the EPC and WP-3 have changed over the years.

Their most important new task: to serve as intellectual crucibles in which policy is forged for the annual G-7 summit.

Over the years, the two bodies have drawn the world's economic gurus. Renowned central bankers like Italy's Guido Carli, Germany's Hans Tietmeyer and France's Jacques de Larosière have been among its members. Emile van Lennep, later to serve as OECD Secretary-General, chaired both groups. It was also served by OECD policy-framers, brilliant economists, like John Fay, Stephen Marris, Sylvia Ostry, Jeffrey Shafer and John Llewellyn.

A full list of chairs of these two key economic bodies follows:

Chairs of the Economic Policy Committee

1959	Sir Hugh Ellis-Rees (United Kingdom)
1960-1965	Lord Hankey (United Kingdom)
1965-1968	Sir Edgar Cohen (United Kingdom)
1969	Emile van Lennep (Netherlands)
1970-1971	Emile van Lennep (Netherlands)
1972-1977	Sir Douglas Allen (United Kingdom)
1978-1980	Charles L. Schultze (United States)
1981-1982	Murray Wiedenbaum (United States)
1982	Sir Douglas Wass (United Kingdom)
1983-1984	Martin Feldstein (United States)
1985-1988	Beryl Sprinkel (United States)
1989	Michael J. Boskin (United States)
1990	Bernhard Molitor (Germany)
	Michael J. Boskin (United States)

1991	Bernhard Molitor
	(Germany)
1992	Michael J. Boskin
	(United States)
	Bernhard Molitor
	(Germany)
1993	Bernhard Molitor
	(Germany)
	Laura Tyson
	(United States)
1994	Laura Tyson
	(United States)
	Alan Budd
	(United Kingdom)
	Tsutomo Tanaka (Japan)
1995	Alan Budd
	(United Kingdom)
	Tsutomo Tanaka (Japan)
	Joseph Stiglitz
	(United States)
1996	Joseph Stiglitz
	(United States)

Chairs of Working Party No. 3

1961-1969	Emile van Lennep
	(Netherlands)
1969-1977	Otmar Emminger
	(Germany)
1977-1979	Michiya Matsukawa
	(Japan)
1980-1985	Christopher W. McMahon
	(United Kingdom)
1986-1988	Sir Geoffrey Littler
	(United Kingdom)
1988-1989	Toyoo Gyohten (Japan)
1990-1993	Hans Tietmeyer
	(Germany)
1993-1994	Andrew Crockett
	(United Kingdom)
1994-1996	Larry Summers
	(United States)

Top to bottom, left to right: Charles Schultze; Beryl Sprinkel (USA); Bernhard Molitor (Germany); Hans Tietmeyer (Germany); Toyoo Gyoten (Japan); Lawrence H. Summers (USA); Sir Douglas Allen (UK); Laura Tyson (USA); Lord Hankey (UK); German Finance Minister Helmut Schmidt; Valéry Giscard-d'Estaing, G-10 Chair, March 1973; Dr Joseph E. Stiglitz (USA)

Chapter V

A Day in the Life of a Château

Château de la Muette

A Day in the Life
of a Château

27 February, 1997.

6.20 A.M.   Dawn is still an hour off. Early-rising sparrows chirp merrily in anticipation of a new day. A full moon floats over the Paris horizon as Françoise Fuzier arrives at 2, rue André-Pascal. She nods to the guard on duty, enters the courtyard and descends into the tunnel that leads to 19, rue de Franqueville. The *New Building* of the Organisation for Economic Co-operation and Development is deserted.

In Fuzier's ground-floor office, the morning newspapers await her, *Libération* and *Les Échos* together with the *International Herald Tribune*, the *Financial Times* and the *Wall Street Journal*. But – *zut!* – one of her teleprinters has run out of paper. She will call the French wire service, Agence France-Presse, for a repeat of material she has missed.

Today, Fuzier leads her 60-page press review with three versions of a speech by Alan Greenspan, Chairman of the US Federal Reserve Board, warning that American interest rates could rise soon. An assistant who arrives at 7 A.M. clips the stories Fuzier marks. At 8.40, the package goes to the printer in the basement. At 9 A.M., the first printed copy reaches the desk of Donald Johnston, the OECD Secretary-General. By 10 A.M., 450 copies of the press review have been delivered to officials throughout the Organisation and to the delegation offices of its 29 member states.

6.30 A.M. Genevieve McInnes places a call from her home phone to the Environment Ministry in Canberra. Because of the ten-hour time difference, this is the hour to do it. (Most days, she corresponds with the Australian capital through e-mail.) The deadline is looming for the Environment directorate's first *Environmental Performance Report* on Australia, which McInnes is drafting. Among other things, she is writing about the harm done to Australia's bio-diversity by such "exotic species" as rabbits and foxes. Other issues include pollution, ecosystems, sustainable development, mining.

7.40 A.M. Im Hong Jae, counsellor at the Korean delegation to OECD, lives five minutes away from his office. He believes that the early bird catches the worm. Im reads overnight cables, briefs his Ambassador and drives to the Château for today's Council meeting. Once again, he is early: "timeliness conveys the message of not being a late-comer." For most of the rest of the day, he sits at his ambassador's elbow, following the debate with passionate interest. Back at delegation headquarters at 5 P.M., he prepares and drafts a detailed report on the Council activities for the government in Seoul and Korean embassies in other OECD countries.

Drafting of the long report takes five hours and Im stresses that it will play an "important role in the Korean government's policy formation process." Moreover, he points out that Korea is "still considered a new member and is still engaged in the learning process."

8.00 A.M. Christopher Brooks is one of a small team assembled by the Secretary-General to reflect on OECD's role in the next millennium. He begins the day at a working breakfast with Lady Shirley Williams, P.C., former British minister, member of the House of Lords and professor at the Kennedy School of Government at Havard University. She is also a long-standing friend of the OECD. Brooks and Williams discuss the process of change in Central and Eastern Europe. Brooks later labours over the file on possible renovation, or move, of the sprawl of OECD buildings in Paris's Sixteenth district.

8.30 A.M. Marie-Lou Gabriel serves *café au lait* and croissants to a succession of groggy OECD personnel. Marie-Lou has been working behind the counter of the sixth-floor snack bar for twenty-five years. She can't imagine going anywhere else. She treats every single customer to a radiant smile and a hearty "*Bonjour*". "Poor things," she laments, "they work so hard they never get a proper lunch."

Marie-Lou provides a host of services beyond just serving coffee. Customers leave messages with her for one another. Others park their baggage and packages. And they show their gratitude in little ways. Yesterday, a retired official dropped by and handed Marie-Lou an envelope full of exotic postage stamps for her children's collections.

8.40 A.M. In Chinese Taipei, ten time-zones away, Michel Potier tucks into the first course of a lavish Chinese banquet hosted by the Taiwan Environmental Agency. (The first course was supposed to have been sharkfin soup; in fact, the soup is on the menu but not in the dish, since sharks are now a protected species). Earlier in the day, Potier, a senior official in OECD's environment directorate, addressed a conference on International Environmental Partnership. Potier is one of dozens of officials scattered about the world today, extending the Organisation's "outreach" to non-member countries.

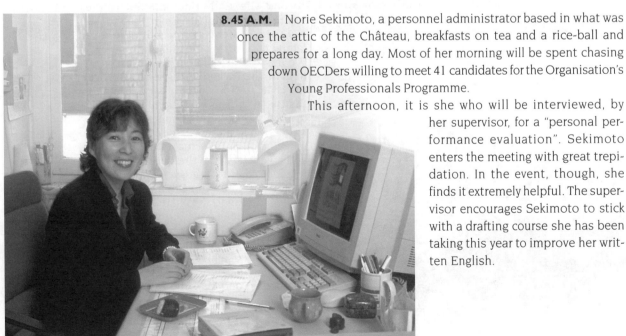

8.45 A.M. Norie Sekimoto, a personnel administrator based in what was once the attic of the Château, breakfasts on tea and a rice-ball and prepares for a long day. Most of her morning will be spent chasing down OECDers willing to meet 41 candidates for the Organisation's Young Professionals Programme.

This afternoon, it is she who will be interviewed, by her supervisor, for a "personal performance evaluation". Sekimoto enters the meeting with great trepidation. In the event, though, she finds it extremely helpful. The supervisor encourages Sekimoto to stick with a drafting course she has been taking this year to improve her written English.

Expérience de la Machine Aérostatique de M. Mongolfier au Château de la Muette, le 21 9bre 1783.

CHÂTEAU DE LA MUETTE

I**T IS** only 75 years old. And it is not really a château – rather the opulent mansion of an extremely wealthy Paris banker. But No. 2, rue André-Pascal, seat of the OEEC and OECD since 1949, is nonetheless an appropriate setting for the "club of rich nations". Vast and comfortable, it lends dignity to international meetings, and it is full of historical associations reaching back to the medieval times.

A horse-shoe shaped structure of strict neo-classical style, the modern-day Château de la Muette was built by Baron Henri de Rothschild between 1915 and 1922. In the 1920s and 1930s, the château housed the famous Rothschild art collections. Its great public rooms – including what is now the OECD's Council room – were the scene of glittering receptions and dinners. During World War II, the German army took over the building and used it as a military headquarters. After the liberation of Paris, it was taken over by the American army. It became the seat of the OEEC in 1949. The first version of the château – a few hundred yards away from the existing building – was very modest, a royal hunting lodge in the middle of what is now the Bois de Boulogne. Its name probably derived from the word "meute," meaning a pack of hunting dogs. In the late Sixteenth Century, King Henri IV transformed the lodge into a small château for his wife, Marguerite de Navarre. Though the king and "Queen Margot" later divorced, she left the property to the son of Henri IV's second wife, Catherine de Médicis: the future King Louis XIII. From 1606 to 1792, the château served both the royal family and, with increasing frequency, the mistresses of kings.

In 1716, the Duchesse de Berry took over the château. The duchess, whose father the Duc d'Orléans was regent during the childhood of King Louis XV, held opulent parties at la Muette, mingling the intellectual élite of the day and aristocrats from the depraved Regency court. At one such reception she hosted Tsar Peter the Great. As king, Louis XV claimed the château for himself; there, the queen gave birth to ten children in ten years. Later in his reign, however, Louis XV used the château mainly to house his many mistresses, including the celebrated Madame de Pompadour and Madame Dubarry.

Louis XVI, who was fated to die by the guillotine during the French Revolution, spent the happiest days of his life at the château with his young Austrian bride, Marie-Antoinette. The royal couple, still vastly popular, would stroll through the surrounding woods – part of the modern Bois de Boulogne – which resounded with cries of "Vive le roi!" In this period, the king granted a patch of sandy ground near the château to Antoine Parmentier, chief apothecary of the French army, who introduced the potato to France. In 1783, the first successful flight of a hot-air balloon was launched from the château gardens, in a craft fashioned by the Montgolfier brothers. Benjamin Franklin attended the launching.

Revolution put an end to royal ownership of the château. Deputies to the radical Constitutional Convention dined in the state chambers. La Fayette rode a white horse into the courtyard to a chorus of cheers. Soon the National Assembly decided to sell the property to the highest bidder. The vast park was subdivided; the château itself passed into the hands of Sebastiani Érard, a wealthy piano manufacturer. In the 1880s, it became the property of the Comte de Franqueville, whose name is preserved in the name of the street bordering the east side of the modern château. In 1912, the de Franqueville family sold out; further subdividing occurred, making room for one of the poshest residential developments in Paris. Today, the château is a place of strong contrasts. The smoothly manicured gardens are dotted with utilitarian Quonset huts. The servants' quarters in the eaves have been converted into offices for OECD's personnel staff. Computers and office furniture stand where priceless Eighteenth Century furniture once gleamed.

But the grand old building maintains some of its former glory, especially the magnificent marble-floored entry hall and the majestic staircase that sweeps up to the first or "noble" floor. A special stateliness attaches to the vast Council room, where the ambassadors of member countries regularly meet to oversee the activities of the Organisation for Economic Co-operation and Development.

9.30 A.M. In Meeting Room No. 3 of the New Building, experts and officials gather to review international standards for agricultural tractors. At the same time, in Room No. 1, more than 100 representatives of member states begin hard bargaining over a proposed Multilateral Agreement on Investment (MAI in English; AMI – the word for "friend" – in French). These are just two of the 19 OECD meetings, consultations, seminars and negotiating sessions (including the Council) scheduled for today.

10.00 A.M. Meetings, meetings, meetings. Two miles away from the Château, on the other side of the Seine, Robert Priddle, Executive Director of the International Energy Agency, ploughs into a solid day of in-house consultations. IEA, an autonomous body within the OECD framework, moved recently from the New Building to the Australian Embassy, a modern, crescent-shaped structure near the Eiffel Tower. Priddle's first meeting, with his office directors, produces discussion of the energy situation around the Caspian Sea and in Brazil.

The same group reassembles a bit later to work on the first draft of a communiqué for the IEA Ministerial meeting in May. (By tradition the IEA meeting is held every second year, just before the OECD Ministerial.) After a sandwich lunch in his office, Priddle chairs still another internal meeting, this one on preparations for a United Nations conference on climate change to be held in Kyoto in December. Later this evening, he will dine with the president of the European Investment Bank.

10.10 A.M. Johnston enters the large, airy Council room. Earlier, the Secretary-General has huddled with Eric Burgeat, Andrew Dean and Elizabeth Dickson, his closest aides, reviewing a speech on Marshall Plan that Johnston will deliver two days hence. He noted that the draft contains no reference to key European leaders of the period: Georges Bidault, Ernest Bevin, Robert Schuman. The names are inserted.

Ambassadors from all member countries and the European Union are seated around three sides of a large square composed of long modern tables. Johnston sits on the fourth side with Joanna Shelton, a Deputy Secretary-General, to his right; and Roger Harmel, Secretary of the Council, taking notes and advising on his left. Each ambassador is accompanied by two or three aides. Three rows of straight chairs are filled with directors and experts from the Secretariat.

The meeting opens with the ringing of a handbell.

Johnston reports on his activities of the past two weeks. The Secretariat has been working on "many aspects of the reform" of the Organisation. The President of Estonia has visited Johnston, pushing his country's candidacy for membership; Johnston was not in a position to make the Estonian any promises, but, he said, "there is no moratorium on new members". The Secretary-General has delivered a speech in Düsseldorf. He has taken part in a "frank" brainstorming session with the private Business and Industry Association accredited to the OECD.

"We want the views from people who are on the line"

Then Johnston speaks of his efforts to shape the OECD's future. An elaborate "prioritisation exercise" is under way, aimed at making the Organisation's work more focused. The directors of all OECD Directorates are involved, because "we want the views from people who are on the line". At the same time, a small team formed by Johnston is studying views from the Council and OECD committees, the results of a similar review done in 1995, as well as papers by Johnston himself and by his predecessor Jean-Claude Paye.

In the tradition of Canadian politicians, Johnston alternates between French and English. Ms. Shelton, an American, does the same as she reports on a workshop she attended in Brasilia on the MAI involving fourteen Latin American countries. "The Brazilians are taking a serious look at this," she says.

Jean-Jacques Noreau, the OECD Executive Director, briefs the Council on the possible move of OECD headquarters across Paris. A study of the issue is under way.

An ambassador upends the plaque bearing his country's name. This gesture is known as "putting up your flag"; it means you are asking for the floor. He wants a cost estimate on studies for possible sites for the OECD.

Then the ambassadors discuss plans for the Ministerial meeting scheduled in May. Johnston suggests that the traditional long, dull *communiqué* be made more "punchy." "The *communiqué* in its traditional form," Johnston remarks, "has never been a best-seller with the press."

The Council recesses at 1.10 P.M.

Johnston and Estonian President Lennart Merri

11.00 A.M. At her office in the Château, Alexandra Trzeciak-Duval receives a ranking official from Mongolia. The Mongolian wants to know how OECD decisions are made on country programmes. He also wants to discuss the Organisation's forthcoming *Investment Guide to Mongolia*, which will be launched at a World Bank meeting in Ulan Bator in June. He asks how export financing schemes work. Trzeciak-Duval directs her visitor to a number of "off-the-shelf" documents on export financing and to the OECD Internet site, where a large amount of information is readily available.

As chief of the Russian desk in the Centre for Co-operation with Economies in Transition, Trzeciak-Duval oversees 25 separate activities in that country. Today she checks on a Russian request for observer status in an OECD expert group. She calls Johnston to brief him on the approaching visit of a high Russian official. She spends an hour on a project involving a regional approach to restructuring in Siberia.

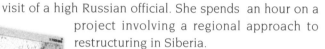

1.00 P.M. Bernard "Joe" Phillips signs off on the final draft of a speech that the Secretary-General will give next Monday at a conference on electronic commerce. Phillips is chief of the Consumer and Competition division of the Financial Fiscal and Enterprise Affairs directorate ("Daffy", in OECD argot).

Phillips has spent much of the morning polishing the speech. But he has also:

- read about 80 of the 120 e-mail messages in his computer;
- discussed financing for two missions next month, one to Bangkok, the other to New Delhi;
- spoken with a British diplomat about next week's Consumer Policy meeting;
- revised a paper on a conference on the cost of international parcel delivery;
- made travel arrangements for the New Delhi trip;
- volunteered to help draft the Ministerial report on regulatory reform.

And that's not the end of it. After a 20-minute lunch break, Phillips:

- confers with Eric Burgeat about the electronic commerce conference;
- calls a co-worker on mission in Mexico;
- speaks with a Canadian diplomat;
- tries to reach an American official, fails, talks with her assistant;
- edits the executive summary of a forthcoming report and finds that a virus has infected 33 files in his computer – including the Johnston speech;
- speaks with a Korean diplomat;
- attends a farewell party for a member of his division who is retiring, where Phillips talks electronics with a Japanese diplomat and talks shop with a colleague who warns him to be wary of a certain consultant.

At 9.30 P.M., he arrives for dinner at the home of friends, an hour and a half late.

3.00 P.M. Controlled panic in the Analytical Data Base section of the Department of Economics. An hour from now, Portia Eltvedt is to present "Econet," a newly-devised subdivision of OECD's existing "Intranet" system, before a group of in-house VIPs. Econet will carry items of special interest to the Organisation's Economics Department. Eltvedt has designed a colourful PC-activated screen presentation that is continually updated with new images.

After a sandwich and mineral-water lunch at her desk, Eltvedt arranges to include snatches of Alan Greenspan's 10 A.M. speech in Washington (4 P.M. in Paris). The OECD directors applaud the demonstration – especially the Greenspan part.

No rest for the weary. Eltvedt returns to her desk to find an urgent message saying that her "mission report" on a recent trip to Washington is due. So are data for the spring round of forecasting for all OECD member countries. "How can data be dull," Eltvedt asks, "when we are on the edge of catastrophe?"

3.10 P.M. The Council meeting resumes, with Johnston in the chair.

Ambassadors continue their discussion of the coming Ministerial meeting. One asks: "Why should ministers come all the way to Paris to give a canned four-minute speech before an empty room?" A consensus emerges around "a new formula" for the session – a "real open debate."

Jean-Jacques Noreau outlines to the Council an agreement with the OECD Staff Association covering compensation for 45 employees made redundant to meet the down-sizing targets necessitated by the Organisation's shrinking budget. The staff cuts and another 40 posts eliminated by attrition sparked uncharacteristic complaints and demonstrations by the OECD Staff Association. It took three months of tough bargaining to achieve an accord, which is finally approved by the Council.

With the redundancy issue resolved, the Council is in a position to approve the OECD budget for the current year. It does so with a collective sigh of relief. The Organisation, which has for years been pushing governments to make painful structural adjustments, is now engaged in that very process; the 1997 budget is 3 per cent lower than that of the previous year.

A series of measures that have already received approval from the Council's Executive Committee are passed rapidly. A discussion develops about Chinese participation in one of the OECD dialogue programmes. Beyond the issue on the table lies the much larger question of OECD relations with China over the longer term.

Council adjourns a little after 5 P.M.

Johnston rushes to his office to talk with participants in the committee on Information, Computer and Communications Policy, which is meeting this week.

Johnston discusses a speech with his aides: from left, Andrew Dean, Johnston, Gabriella Goekjian, Eric Burgeat, Elizabeth Dickson

3.15 P.M. Two weeks ago, Carl Wahren, of the OECD's Development Co-operation Directorate, gave a talk at a Paris church on issues of global survival. To his amazement, a member of the audience – a journalist from a well-known Catholic publication – took his ideas seriously and has asked to follow them up.

The reporter sits in Wahren's office in one of the Quonset huts and peppers him with sincere, searching questions. "What will globalisation do for the poorest of the poor? For the least developed countries? Is the Western development model itself sustainable? And what about injustice? Gender inequality? Water scarcity? Will the Market take care of all these?" Wahren replies as best he can. But the visit leads him to search his own soul. He recalls T.S. Eliot's lines:

> "We are all looking for systems so perfect
> That no one will have to be good…"

"We are all looking for systems so perfect, that no one will have to be good…"

3.45 P.M. Madeleine Walter spends most working days inside a glassed-in panel overlooking an OECD meeting room. She is one of 16 conference interpreters who keep the Organisation bilingual. Today she is working on the MAI negotiations. It is a difficult assignment, with dozens of background documents to be mastered. But Walter is fascinated by the process; she was present at the creation of MAI, at a 1995 conference. "Two years later," she says, "they still haven't found a definition for "investment". (Very shortly after this session, the ultra-elusive definition is finally adopted.)

There are four interpreters working each booth. They spell one another in half-hour shifts. It is intricate, arduous work, but there are some light moments too. One delegate delights the interpreters with his endlessly mixed metaphors: "This glass is half full," he is fond of saying. "We need to put some flesh on its bones."

4.00 P.M. Eileen Capponi, an assistant in the Statistics Directorate, fields a question from a subscriber to the diskette version of the Organisation's best-selling *Main Economic Indicators*. Could he, the caller asks, receive the *Economic Outlook* on a diskette with the same software as on the MEI diskette? Capponi has been asked the same question before. Happily, the answer is "Yes". The client can import all the data from both publications into his home database without using the presentation software.

4.20 P.M. It has been one of those days for Ronald Steenblik, of the Agricultural Directorate. Late to work. Unable to log onto the computer network, which refuses his new password. He is finishing up a paper on *Fisheries Adjustment: Accompanying Social and Labour Policies in Selected Member Countries."* Everybody Steenblik needs to talk to seems to be out of the office. No answer at the International Social Security Association in Geneva. An expert Steenblik knows at the IEA has gone home to Canada. His contact at the maritime industries branch of the International Labour Organisation is on mission in Malta! What's more, his computer keeps crashing.

Finally, though, persistence pays off. Steenblik receives a fax from the ILO that provides much of the information he needs. He settles down to drafting his paper, pretty much without interruptions. At 6.30, he calls it a day; it's his son's third birthday.

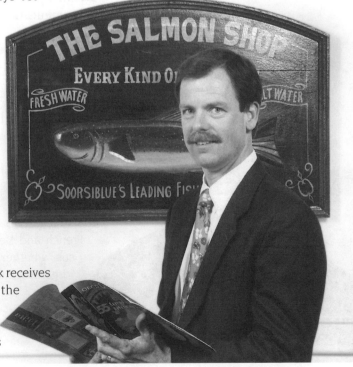

5.00 P.M. The MAI negotiating session in Room No. 1 has sailed into rough waters. In principle, the negotiations are to be completed in two-and-a-half months, for submission to the May ministerial meeting. But today's session indicates that deadline may be a bit optimistic.

One delegation after another expresses reservations: points in the proposed agreement on which they would seek specific exceptions. One country's legislation does not permit foreigners to own fishing boats. Another excludes cabotage by foreign ships. A number of countries have "golden share" arrangements to protect key industries from foreign take-over. Finland, Norway and Sweden want an exception to protect the Sami people (Lapps) from competition in reindeer breeding.

Literally hundreds of reservations have been tabled. Frans Engering, the Dutch official chairing the negotiations, urges participants to rethink their positions overnight. Unless a fresh approach to the whole issue of "country-specific reservations" is found quickly, work on this very crucial element of the agreement could well drag on beyond the May deadline.

5.30 P.M. At a meeting of the Information, Communications and Computer Policy Committee in Room No. 2, John Dryden, an expert on Internet issues in the Secretariat, takes notes. Belgium and France offer tough proposals for policing the content of the Internet. Belgium, traumatised by the discovery of a large paedophile network on its territory, wants to ban material on sex with children. France's suggestion is broader, including a code of conduct that would ban, among other things, Nazi and neo-Nazi propaganda.

Other delegations express sympathy for the French and Belgian concerns and discuss whether the OECD is the proper organisation to address them.

Michèle Rigaud teaches OECD staffers how to improve their communication skills. Today, her office has organised three separate courses. This morning, in the house cinema, 75 people attended a session on the Organisation's Internet policies. An all-day course for non-native English speakers on report-writing in English has just wound up. (OECD is a major purveyor of training in French and English, and results are excellent, although some callers are surprised by the heavy British Midlands accent that prevails at the OECD. The reason: a very popular CD-ROM called *Telephoning in English*, in which the model accent is distinctly "North of London".)

Now Rigaud checks in at the end of a special session for English-speaking officials on how to run a recruitment panel. The seven "students" are assigned roles as job-candidates or examiners, and they are filmed as they play those parts. When the videos are replayed, these scenes are greeted with whoops of incredulous and embarrassed laughter, as the candid camera victims witness their own behaviour.

7.50 P.M. Johnston breaks off a meeting to attend a goodbye party for a secretary who is leaving OECD to spend a year in China. By popular request, the Secretary-General, who is an enthusiastic pianist, sits down at the ivories and pounds out a medley of songs for the guest of honour. Among them: *I've Grown Accustomed to Her Face* from *My Fair Lady* and the classic Beatles' ballad that begins: *Something in the way she moves.* Johnston then returns to his office and his talk with his aides. He leaves for home at 9.15.

10.15 P.M. Janet West and Steve Cutts, of the Trade Directorate, wind up work on yet another reform package for negotiation by participants in the Arrangement on Guidelines for Officially Supported Export Credits. The punishing task of reducing state subsidies seems absolutely endless.

11.00 P.M. The phone rings at home for Genevieve McInnes. It's a New Zealand official working on his own environmental performance review. The time is 11 A.M. in Auckland.

11.30 P.M. After his marathon day of Council attendance and report writing, Im Hong Jae turns out the lights at the Korean delegation office and heads home. Officials in Seoul are already reading his report.

Midnight The Château is shut and dark. Here and there at Franqueville and in the Quonset hut complexes a lonely light burns on. One or two officials still have calls to make to impossible time zones. Negotiators on the MAI continue to hammer out new language, among themselves and with their capitals.
Another – fairly average – day in the life of the OECD is history.

Chapter VI

Innovation as a Way of Life

The Thinker, by Auguste Rodin

Innovation
as a Way of Life

CALL **it pioneering. Or innovation. Trail-blazing or creativity. Call it staying ahead of the curve. By whatever name, OECD's stock in trade, its ultimate reason for being, is its capacity to anticipate looming problems and to propose novel solutions.**

The Organisation's creation was, in itself, an act of radical innovation – designed by its visionary fathers to deal with the unprecedented destruction and economic paralysis caused by World War II. Its first decade saw the emergence of a long run of original institutions and policy approaches: a productivity agency, a payments union, a nuclear energy agency. It pioneered an entirely new approach to the gathering and treatment of economic statistics.

Innovation continued through the years of postwar prosperity and into the stormy 1970's and 1980's. OECD's responses to the two oil shocks and to the collapse of Communism were characteristically innovative. These were also the years when the Organisation was pioneering international co-operation on environmental issues. In conjunction with the General Agreement on Tariffs and Trade (forerunner of the World Trade Organisation), it was finding ways to extend and liberate commerce worldwide. Its statisticians were working on the revolutionary notion of "purchasing power parity," which, for the first time, made possible meaningful comparisons of individual well-being from one country to another.

The process is by no means complete. In virtually every area of the Organisation's work, pioneering policy approaches are being developed or put into place. Advanced (some even futuristic) theories are under study. OECD experts are looking toward the near and distant future.

In an era of sustained growth and political stability, the primary ill that continues to plague the economies of many member governments is high unemployment, especially among young people. In 1994, OECD published a massive Jobs Study which analysed the causes of unemployment and suggested a series of innovative measures to fight it. The study, which was praised as the most comprehensive ever done, has become the basis for new employment legislation and practices in a number of member countries. Three years after its publication, it remains among the most visible and influential of OECD's current activities. (**see Box page 100**)

It is, however, just one in a very long list:

AGEING POPULATIONS

Dramatic shifts in the demographic patterns of OECD member countries carry the seeds of what some OECD experts describe as "a coming catastrophe, the magnitude of which can't be over-estimated." In 1996, the Organisation published *Ageing in OECD Countries: A Critical Policy Challenge*. While much of the rest of the world worries about rapidly rising populations, Europe, Japan and to a lesser extent North America have seen birth rates tumble in the past two decades, while life expectancy continues to rise.

In countries like Germany and Italy, where current birth rates have dropped below the replacement level, pension costs will rise steeply during the next few decades. A falling number of active workers will bear the burden of supporting an increasing number of retirees. More frail and elderly people will require more and more expensive care from their families and from health services. Labour markets, now glutted, will be hard-pressed to find the highly-skilled employees that increasingly technological economies will need. Policies will have to be developed to provide healthy senior citizens with meaningful and useful activities.

These are huge issues, and the OECD work does not presume to resolve them all. But it points urgently to the narrow window of opportunity between now and the year 2020 during which governments and the private sector can prepare for the coming demographic upheaval. It offers a long list of policy orientations, including the controversial recommendation that the age of retirement be raised in most OECD countries, and raised soon. It calls for a reorientation of medical-care priorities to accommodate an increasing demand for chronic care facilities. Perhaps its most interesting and original insight is the notion of "active ageing", involving the retraining of citizens late in life and the provision of tasks where they can use their acquired experience to the advantage of all. Like the *Jobs Study* and most of the other activities mentioned here, OECD's ongoing work on the issues of ageing will extend over many years. It will continue to draw on expertise from a variety of the Organisation's directorates: from economists to experts on fiscal matters, social policy and many others. Through its committees, it will also involve member-country officials from many ministries and departments in a policy process likely to last decades.

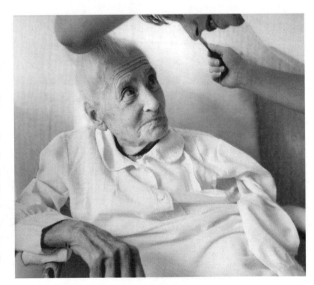

TRADE ISSUES

The completion of the Uruguay Round of world-wide trade negotiations at the end of 1993 transformed the face of international commerce. For the first time ever, it applied enforce-able multilateral rules to trade in agriculture, services and intellectual property. The 50-year-old General Agree-ment on Tariffs and Trade, under which the round was held, was renamed the World Trade Organisation and given greatly enlarged powers to settle disputes among the parties.

Successful completion of the Uruguay Round depended to a critical degree on trail-blazing work done in OECD on the measurement of agricultural subsidies, using the concept of Producer Subsidy Equivalents. For years, the United States and the European Union, the two largest agricultural powers, had accused one another of lavishing subsidies on their farmers. But no one really knew how much – until OECD worked out, product by product, the exact amounts involved. The work was an authentic success story, the creative application of statistical and economic expertise to unsnarl a real-world problem of huge proportions.

In addition to their work on farm subsidies, the Organisation's trade experts also pushed the view that trade in services, which now account for a far larger share of the world's wealth, should be brought under GATT rules. Much of the analytical and conceptual basis of the contentious negotiation that finally produced a Uruguay Round agreement took place not in Geneva but in OECD committees.

But the Uruguay Round was not the end of the story, not at any rate in the OECD view. Rapid globalisation of the world economy has brought to the fore a new set of trade issues that may be taken up in successive rounds. OECD teams are at work on such previously exotic topics as the links between trade and competition policy and trade and the environment, breaking ground for negotiations that may not come about for several years. When officials do meet, however, they will draw on the foundation of knowledge and analysis meticulously compiled by OECD experts.

(In a break with usual practice, OECD analysis suggested that one controversial subject need *not* become part of future trade agreements: the issue of trade and labour standards. Several OECD member states have argued that some developing countries unfairly use cheap and unprotected labour to undercut prices in world markets. After an exhaustive study, the Organisation judged that the trade advantage achieved through low core labour standards was trivial. That was an unexpected finding for many. Using objective analytical tools, OECD experts knocked down a widely-held piece of conventional wisdom and thereby set the stage for a better informed – and possibly less heated – discussion.)

European investment in Asia

Bhopal, India

THE MULTILATERAL AGREEMENT ON INVESTMENT

In a globalising economy, trade and investment issues are closely linked. And the level of international investment is rising at a breakneck pace, the majority of it from – and into – OECD countries. "Firms invest to trade and trade to invest," as OECD Secretary-General Donald Johnston puts it.

Ministers of the Organisation decided at their annual meeting in May, 1995, to move beyond the existing OECD codes liberalising capital movements and invisible business transactions and to negotiate a formal treaty. The MAI aims for a high degree of market access and legal security for overseas investors. It aims to liberalise conditions for new investments and provide non-discriminatory treatment for existing investments. It seeks to ensure fair compensation in the event an investment is nationalised by the host country. It guarantees the free repatriation of profits. It establishes a dispute settlement procedure similar to the one that exists in WTO.

Signatories to the MAI will include both current OECD members, and, eventually, non-members attracted by the guarantees it provides for their own investments abroad. Negotiating such an agreement is not easy. Nearly every OECD country sought exceptions for certain of its domestic sectors – such as inland navigation, agriculture and even movie production. But the potential benefits of the MAI are so apparent that the heavy work of overcoming obstacles will surely prove worth all the trouble.

Jean-Claude Paye and Spanish Foreign Minister Javier Solana (now Secretary-General of NATO) launching the MAI, 1995

MUTUAL SURVEILLANCE

The name may recall George Orwell's "1984", but in a world that is both increasingly complex and, in some respects, increasingly uniform, it has demonstrated its value as a policy tool. First used in the 1960's in the macroeconomic area, systematic mutual comparison of policy performance has now spread to trade matters, labour practices, environmental standards and a host of other areas.

The basic principle is that policies implemented in one country invariably spill over into others. Co-operative policy-making involving full recognition of interdependence can therefore achieve more than independent action. More colloquially, mutual surveillance can help avoid the application of "beggar-thy-neighbour" policies.

In a sense, the Bretton Woods system of fixed but adjustable exchange rates that prevailed from the end of World War II till the early 1970's was the grand-daddy of all multilateral surveillance systems. Since Bretton Woods broke down, the procedure has grown more sophisticated; it is no longer based on rules but on general agreements among countries about primary policy goals, like the avoidance of inflation. It is backed up by batteries of statistics such as those available in the OECD's *Main Economic Indicators*. Where the focus of the technique was once on such straightforward benchmarks as trade surpluses and deficits, it is now used to compare much more complex indicators, such as trade-distorting subsidies.

With countries like China, Brazil and India emerging as major players on the world economic stage, the OECD predicts that they will gradually be integrated into the surveillance process. At the same time, the process will extend to more and more substantive areas. And it will continue to enhance OECD's "comparative advantage" as a centre of co-ordination for national policies across the whole spectrum of policy concerns.

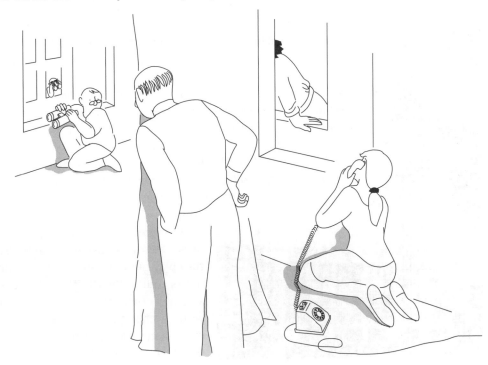

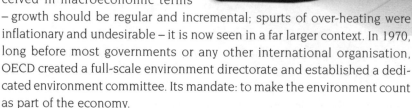

SUSTAINABLE DEVELOPMENT

This notion has gained pertinence and visibility throughout the life of the Organisation. Originally conceived in macroeconomic terms – growth should be regular and incremental; spurts of over-heating were inflationary and undesirable – it is now seen in a far larger context. In 1970, long before most governments or any other international organisation, OECD created a full-scale environment directorate and established a dedicated environment committee. Its mandate: to make the environment count as part of the economy.

Since then, the Organisation has stayed on the leading edge of the effort to reconcile growth in trade, production and wealth with the preservation of the environment. Other OECD bodies, notably the agriculture, development co-operation, transport and science and industry directorates, have collaborated in dozens of sustainable development projects. A recent focus has been the issue of trade and the environment.

PUBLIC MANAGEMENT

Globalisation has wrested control of much national policy away from national governments. Economic interdependence and global news media have "internationalised" issues that were traditionally "home matters". War and famine in Ethiopia are more visible and transparent than ever before. Interest groups, such as ethnic minorities and anti-smokers, routinely organise along trans-national lines. Regional groupings like the European Union and Asean are claiming elements of their members' national sovereignty.

OECD's central brief is economic, but problems of governance have become so inextricably internationalised that the Organisation has become deeply involved in them. Indeed, Donald Johnston, the current Secretary-General, describes "good governance" as one of the three essential elements of a balanced international system (along with economic growth and social stability).

This work is mind-bendingly wide-ranging. It includes studies of the impact of regional organisations, regulatory co-operation and some of the trickiest of the cyberspace issues. OECD experts are advising member governments on how to achieve greater accountability and openness. They are studying the same issues as they play out in international fora (including, of course, the OECD itself). Here, as in so many other areas of the Organisation's work, a changing world environment is evoking innovative responses to problems that scarcely existed a decade ago.

REGULATORY REFORM

It is a truism that regulations are the most down-to-earth and immediate expression of government authority. Regulations are essential, but they can contain unnecessary red tape and are often designed to solve yesterday's problems in today's world. OECD has launched a vast study aimed at developing overarching policy goals in this area backed by extensive recommendations. The central aim is to ensure that national regulations are framed in such a way as to promote competition and market forces, not frustrate them. Telecommunications, professional services, electricity, financial services, agro-food and product standards were among the first areas of regulation to be taken up at OECD.

This initiative is not only pioneering, it challenges member governments to adapt their practices in areas long considered purely national to meet international norms and advance international goals. A follow-through programme is expected to last for several years.

FIGHTING BRIBERY AND CORRUPTION

Along with offering global opportunities, globalisation facilitates global crime, international bribery and corruption. In 1994, OECD governments agreed to a general Recommendation under which they resolved to take concrete acts against bribery. In 1996, they committed themselves to re-examine their fiscal regulations with a view to eliminating tax deductions for bribes paid to foreign officials. (Only the United States, under its Foreign Corrupt Practices Act, already disallowed such deductions.) A number of countries favour making such payments a criminal act, but others are reticent.

"All these issues need resolution, but the game is certainly worth the candle"

Like many of OECD's leading-edge projects, the campaign against international bribery poses daunting intellectual problems. What is a bribe? Does it necessarily involve a breach of duty on the part of the official receiving it? How to handle the issue of extra-territoriality? Must the bribe be offered within the boundaries of the briber's country? All these issues need resolution, but the game is certainly worth the candle. According to the American Commerce Department, US businesses lost 100 overseas deals worth $45 billion because of bribery by foreign competitors – all in a recent two-year period.

Progress on the issue has been incremental, and much slower than some countries would have liked. But progress there has been. The International Chamber of Commerce and the European Union have both joined OECD in the effort, and several governments have already taken steps to eliminate tax-deductibility for overseas bribes.

INFORMATION AND COMMUNICATION TECHNOLOGIES

This is the Internet decade. It may be the prologue to an Internet century. At any event, issues involving the globalisation of information and communication (ICT) have shot to the top of the OECD agenda. A whole host of directorates are now involved in studying the opportunities and problems involved in creating a Global Information Infrastructure (GII) and managing a Global Information Society (GIS).

Spurred on by the Group of Seven's interest in these issues, OECD committees and experts are now studying both the dazzling opportunities and the myriad of problems raised by the prospect of a worldwide, integrated electronic web. The *Communications Outlook* publication, modeled on its *Economic Outlook*, is replete with statistics and analysis of regulatory developments in member countries, as well as telecommunications

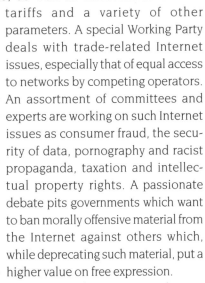

tariffs and a variety of other parameters. A special Working Party deals with trade-related Internet issues, especially that of equal access to networks by competing operators. An assortment of committees and experts are working on such Internet issues as consumer fraud, the security of data, pornography and racist propaganda, taxation and intellectual property rights. A passionate debate pits governments which want to ban morally offensive material from the Internet against others which, while deprecating such material, put a higher value on free expression.

This area of the OECD's work is so close to the state of the art that it changes literally from month to month.

CRYPTOGRAPHY

Of all the ground-breaking projects currently underway in OECD, none is more technical or seemingly mysterious than the work being done on cryptography.

What is it? The standard definition is the techniques that "transform data in order to hide its content, establish its authenticity, prevent its undetected modification or unauthorised use". It is a direct descendant of the encoding or "encryption" developed to protect information sent back to earth from satellites (as well as the targeting directions in military rockets). Now, it is becoming a key element in the Global Information Infrastructure that is rapidly a-building.

Cryptography's obvious use is to preserve the privacy of communications, but it can be applied to a host of other purposes. A cryptographic "signature" can guarantee the receiver of a message that it comes from the proper source. Cryptographic techniques, combined with an electronic payments system, could ensure writers and musicians of being paid by those who enjoy their work on the world-wide web. Soon, parties will be able to sign legal contracts at great distances, in cryptographised cyberspace. But the technique carries dangers as well; it could be used by criminals or terrorists to hide their activities.

Several other organisations are studying cryptography, but OECD has emerged as the preferred forum for officials to discuss the legal and social implications of this chunk of science fiction suddenly become reality.

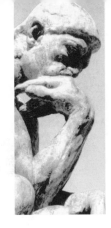

OUTREACH

Not so much a single category of innovation as the very environment in which OECD now lives: OECD remains, as it always has been, a window on the developing world.

Created to deal with a purely European issue – postwar reconstruction – OECD finds itself a major economic player in a world in dizzying transition. The traditional "rich countries'" share of overall wealth is decreasing. Dynamic small nations in Southeast Asia and elsewhere are turning in spectacular productivity performances. Huge, but traditionally poor nations are emerging as possible major actors. The former Communist countries of Eastern and Central Europe as well as the successor republics to the ex-Soviet Union are evolving free-market economies – but at dramatically different rates. Some developing countries remain tragically dependent on Western aid; some are on the point of economic take-off.

If it is to retain the relevance it has enjoyed for half a century, OECD needs to offer appropriate, differentiated responses to all these countries. It must learn from all of them. It must consider accepting some of them as future members. It must offer advice to others, involve still others in parts of its work. It is doing all these things.

"Outreach", as the process has long been known, involves every directorate and division of the Organisation almost every day. OECD experts are "on mission" to the far ends of the globe. Brazilian and Malaysian officials and delegates from scores of other countries, come to Paris for seminars on subjects ranging from taxation to bio-ethics. Specialised groups like the Centre for Co-operation with the Economies in Transition (the ex-Communist countries) and the Club du Sahel (West Africa) have amassed expertise in the problems of specific regions. OECD experts on export credits are at work in Moscow, environmentalists in Beijing.

Through its dense web of linkages, the Organisation constantly reinvents its role in a constantly changing world.

Buenos Aires (top); market in Mali

AN INNOVATIVE PROCESS

By no means the least innovative aspect of OECD is the way in which it operates day by day. Unlike WTO and many other international organisations, OECD has neither a regulatory nor a dispute-settlement function

although it does occasionally negotiate agreements. Unlike NATO, it has no army. Unlike the World Bank and the IMF, it has no money to lend or invest. It exists solely to aid its member states to develop public policy. Uniquely, it both reports to its membership and involves member countries in the analytical process.

To this end, it has developed two specific techniques to nurture creativity. They are OECD's unparalleled committee system and a steady commitment to a "multi-disciplinary" approach to policy issues.

Top: Renato Ruggiero (left) WTO Director General and Sir Leon Brittan, 1996 Centre: Michael Wilson, Canada, Minister for International Trade, June 1991 Bottom-left: Dr Bohn-Young Koo, Korea, then Vice-Minister, Science and Technology; and, Jon Gerrard, Canada, Secretary of State, Science, Research and Development, September 1995

Most people think of OECD as the Secretariat, the 2 000 people who work at the Organisation's Paris headquarters. And indeed, it is this distinguished body which conducts research, compiles and compares statistics and produces 350 publications every year. But the Secretariat is only half the story. The other half consists of the thousands of national officials who compose some 200 OECD committees and working groups. These officials pose the questions that drive the studies, provide the "raw data" for the analysis, develop policy recommendations from the results and are, in a sense, the primary "consumers" of the product. In the end, also, they are the decision-makers who translate the Secretariat's recommendations into real-world policy. Sometimes this takes the form of common undertakings reached within an OECD setting. Just as often, there is no formal agreement, but officials return to their capitals with an enhanced understanding of their colleagues' thinking and with ideas that will find their way into national legislation or regulations.

An innocent-sounding device, but the fact is that OECD committees do serve as a crucible for members' future actions. In the relative privacy of the Organisation's committee rooms, tough issues can be "pre-negotiated", advanced ideas floated, difficulties ironed out. In the corridors and coffee bars between sessions, officials with similar interests but very different backgrounds meet, argue, forge friendships.

A complex process called "peer pressure" occurs. Subtly but powerfully, ideas and standards advocated by a majority of committee members gain the agreement of all or nearly all and are shaped to account for the views of dissenters. No country likes to feel itself on an entirely different wave-length from all its partners. Ultimately peer pressure makes international co-operation among 29 countries possible.

Then there is the "multi-disciplinary" or "horizontal" approach to complex policy issues that has become the Organisation's hallmark in the past two decades. OECD has battered down the walls between "economic" and "social" problems, between "agriculture" and "environment" issues. From the Jobs Study to its trail-blazing work on the ageing of member-country populations, OECD mobilises experts from half-a-dozen fields.

The Development Co-operation directorate works with the Environment directorate to ensure that aid to poor countries does not aggravate their ecological problems. Science and technology studies enlist economists, statisticians, experts on education and labour. With its small staff (compared with the bureaucracies of many member countries) OECD has the flexibility to shift human resources quickly, to cross the boundaries of traditional disciplines. Few of the new issues confronting the developed democracies exist tidily within the outlines of long-established bureaucratic purviews. OECD can ignore those outlines.

"Horizontality" is, of course, not an end in itself. But if the governments of member states continue to treat new problems in old categories – by assigning them exclusively to one existing ministry or another – little is gained. As time passes, however, OECD nudges governments into taking a broader approach to problems. Where just one government department got involved in a given OECD committee's work, two, three or four now do. Ranking OECD officials like to describe how they introduced a senior bureaucrat from one country's tax department to an equally high official from the same country's department of industry. "If they hadn't come to Paris," the generic story ends, "they might *never* have met."

Had there been no OECD in Paris for them to come to, a vast part of the innovative international co-operation that has taken place over the past 50 years might never have come to pass.

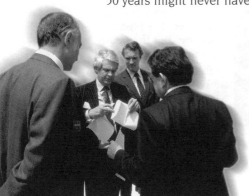

THE *JOBS STUDY:*
AN INTERNATIONAL CASEBOOK

Thirty-six million adult citizens of the world's richest countries have no job. One out of eight Western European "workers" is unemployed. Millions of young people in OECD countries leave school with little hope of finding a reasonably well-paid job. Worse: the plague of unemployment strains the finances of one government after another. The dole absorbs money that might otherwise go to health and education. In an era of low inflation, steadily rising productivity, expanding trade and breakneck technological advance, unemployment remains the one economic problem that the industrialised democracies have failed to solve.

And so it stands at the top of the OECD agenda. In 1992, the Organisation's member countries asked the Secretariat to conduct a massive study of the causes of unemployment, its extent and possible remedies. That effort, published in spring, 1994, as "*The OECD Jobs Study: Facts, Analysis, Strategies*" was quickly adopted by the members as a blue-print for a wide-ranging jobs-creation strategy. It set the agenda for further statistical, analytical and policy-

making activities within the Organisation which will continue and expand well into the next millennium. The *Jobs Study* may one day be seen as among the most valuable pieces of work that OECD has ever done.

It has certainly been one of the most controversial. "A resounding splash," the Reuters news agency reported. "A justification of all the policies we have been following in this country," exulted British Prime Minister John Major. "It uses 50 million unemployed people as an alibi for toughening up the economic system that excludes them," snarled Le Monde diplomatique. "Thanks to unemployment, they'll finally be able to conquer the irreducible enemy: the Welfare State."

That uproar came as no surprise to the scores of experts who worked on the study for nearly two years. Their work pulled few punches. It quickly dismissed the idea that new technology was robbing the OECD countries of jobs. On the contrary, technological advance had produced more jobs than it had destroyed. Equally false, the Study contended, was the protectionist argument that

jobs in the developed world were being lost through competition from low-wage, non-unionised developing countries.

The study noted that the United States had created millions of new jobs over the past decade, but that many of them were ill-paid and carried little, if any, social protection. It pointed to Japan's very low unemployment rate, but cautioned that it concealed a huge amount of uneconomic under-employment. The study reserved its strongest criticism, however, for Continental Europe, where rigidities in the labour market, high minimum wages and unemployment benefits discouraged hiring new workers and made firing them prohibitively expensive.

"Adapt," was the *Jobs Study* authors' key concept. Adapt to technological advance, adapt to the shift from industry to services, adapt to the ineluctable globalisation of trade, technology and culture. Adapt, it warned governments, or reconcile yourselves to high and debilitating jobless rates for decades to come. To achieve that adaptation, the report made 60 separate recommendations that ranged from the macroeconomic (assist recovery through non-inflationary growth) through the practical (promote industry-education partnerships) to the politically incendiary (reduce the dole to make work more attractive than non-work). The study painted a dramatic picture of the "poverty trap"– a contortion of the welfare or tax system in which a worker makes less money by working more.

Controversy over the study rages on. In the past three years, however, it has

spawned tailor-made jobs programmes for each OECD country. These programmes are designed and then monitored by the Organisation. Detailed analysis and policy prescriptions on jobs and joblessness have been added to the periodic *Economic Survey* of each country. Major follow-up studies have been carried out on issues ranging from the effectiveness of active labour-market policies and the interaction between tax and benefit systems, to technology, productivity and job creation. Economists, sociologists and policy experts have combined their skills in the fight against the single most serious problem facing the industrialised world.

The problem will not go away, and it will not be resolved in a short time; indeed, unemployment in the European Union topped 10 per cent and then stuck persistently high. But OECD will continue the struggle, directly and through the actions of its member countries, for as long as it takes.

the Third Millennium

Chapter VII

On to
the Third
Millennium

On to
the Third Millennium

A NEW century, a new millennium, a moment for stock-taking and the summoning of new resolution. For the past 50 years, the OEEC and OECD have responded successfully – sometimes with spectacular success – to the complex and often unexpected challenges that history has presented. The Organisation has guided its members through half a century of unexampled growth and change.

It stimulated the phoenix-like rebirth of Western Europe from the ashes of the world's most awful war. It weathered a sudden quadrupling of basic energy prices and the crippling stagflation that followed. It responded to the chaotic collapse of Communism with a set of imaginative but very practical programmes to help the new democracies to their feet; it has admitted the most successful of the East European countries as full members. It has anticipated and channelled revolutionary developments in economics and society, in agriculture and trade, in biology and computers. It has sensed society's worries about jobs, health, ageing, sustainable growth, and made them part of its policy analysis and advice.

The peoples it serves have prospered beyond the wildest dreams of their fathers and grandmothers. They live longer than ever before and dispose of scientific knowledge that makes the first half of this century seem altogether quaint. OECD has played a significant part in all these developments.

Will the Organisation – can it? – play the same leading-edge role in the third millennium?

Jean-Claude Paye, Deputy Secretary-General Joanna Shelton, Donald Johnston

Not everyone believes it can. Some influential skeptics argue that the
set of international organisations created after World War II – OECD and
NATO, but also the World Bank, the International Monetary Fund and
the UN system in general – have had their day. In the
post-Cold War era, it is suggested, the dinosaurs of   *"Produce more with less"*
the 1940's have become superfluous, even dysfunctional.
Such doubts, however far fetched, have an impact on policy-makers and
legislators. In an era of universal belt-tightening and budget cutting, parlia-
ments have grown stingy with their support to international organisations.
Some countries, including the very largest, have delayed paying their dues.
From nearly every capital comes the demand that OECD, like the others,
"produce more with less."

In the OECD's case, those pressures translated into a 3 per cent budget cut in 1997, with more cuts to come by the year 2000. Eighty-five staff positions were cut in 1996 and 1997, with more to follow. All this in a period when the Organisation is working full-steam on such enormous issues as globalisation and the future effect of new communications technology and the demographic implosion of the West.

A shrinking budget may be the most obvious difficulty in OECD's path. It is not the only one. Just as formidable:

Membership

Should the Organisation remain essentially a homogeneous "club of rich nations"? After admitting Mexico, the Czech Republic, Poland, Hungary and Korea since 1994, should it reach out to embrace the rapidly developing economies of Southeast Asia, Latin America and elsewhere? In the longer term, should it be prepared to admit such huge and very diverse nations as India, China and Russia? If it expands widely and rapidly, will it lose its specificity, its efficiency, its sense of common purpose? If it remains relatively compact, will it not lose its relevance in a world of breakneck change and steadily increasing interdependence?

Procedures

Like the European Union, OECD has realised that the process of expansion requires institutional change. Systems of decision-making and governance that work well in a small organisation with like-minded members become cumbersome, even counter-productive when there are more, and more different, people around the table. Should OECD maintain the rule of consensus (or unanimity), which some members see as a guarantee of sovereignty? Should it switch to majority rule, as the EU is increasingly doing? Does the existing Council – the ultimate decision-making body made up of the ambassadors from member countries – perform optimally as the governing body? Should it be reorganised? Or even dissolved? With what might it be replaced? As with the question of membership, the need to stay relevant will drive decisions about procedures of the future.

Leaders who would not have imagined rapprochement with OECD: Ghandi, Stalin, Mao

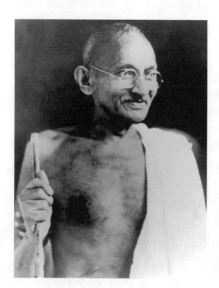

Bazaar, Istanbul

Competition

So far, OECD has managed to avoid duplicating work done in other international fora – sometimes, it must be said, after bitter contests for territory. But the steadily increasing role of the European Union (which contains 15 OECD members) and the World Trade Organisation (which contains them all, plus 115 more countries) as well as several other international bodies, poses the problem afresh. How to avoid situations in which Paris, Brussels and Geneva work separately on a single subject? How to maximise the effectiveness of officials and ministers who must juggle their travel time and a thousand other obligations?

Programme

Over the decades, the Organisation has repeatedly shifted and adapted its focus and its methods to meet the reality of a rapidly changing universe. Conceived to administer a revolutionary post-war recovery programme, it metamorphosed into the policy centre for the world's main industrial democracies. Born into a world of jealous nationalism and narrow protectionism, it steered its membership into the irreversible process of globalisation. Half the subjects discussed at OECD every day – electronic commerce, genetic technology, greying populations, China as a potential world power – were undreamt of at its founding. But is this record sustainable? Can an international institution with fewer than 2 000 people, however brilliant and motivated, continue to serve a growing and increasingly heterogeneous membership in an environment of constant, bewildering change?

Wuhan, China

As Donald Johnston sees it, the world needs the OECD now more than it ever did before.

The very complexity of the current period, he contends, renders the Organisation indispensable. For it is the one body that combines a wealth of analytic expertise with a systematic multi-disciplinary approach to policy problems in an atmosphere of voluntary international co-operation.

Johnston, who took over as Secretary-General on 1 June, 1996, is a new kind of leader for OECD. Neither a European nor a professional civil servant, he brings to the post a Canadian brashness and informality and a politician's preoccupation with building public support for his endeavours. (In an unguarded moment recently, Johnston demonstrated both qualities, remarking: "I want Joe Public in Pittsburgh or Palermo to realise that OECD is working for him.") The Secretary-General was appointed with a mandate to modernise and change the institution and he has a passion to fulfill that mandate.

He has traced new directions for the institution – building on a winning tradition that began with George Marshall's Harvard speech in 1947.

Johnston's first and possibly most decisive innovation was conceptual. It was also unforeseen. As an English-speaker and a North American, he was widely expected to adhere to – even reinforce – the rigorous doctrine of macro-economic and structural adjustment which OECD had embraced throughout the 1980's and 1990's. He did not, of course, reject that tenet. But he did issue a sharp reminder both to member states and to the body of experts he directs that economic efficiencies, entrepreneurship and technological advances were not ends in themselves. The tireless production of wealth was pointless if it did not lead to better lives for ordinary citizens.

Simply stated, Johnston's point was that the aim of economic growth must be social progress.

He outlined a "triangular paradigm," in which economic growth, social stability and "a stable and effective system of governance" form a mutually supportive triad. He has warned of a possibly violent popular "backlash" against too much austerity, too-rapid budget cutting, too little thought for the needs of ordinary citizens.

ECONOMIC
GROWTH

THE
TRIANGULAR
PARADIGM

SOCIAL
STABILITY

GOOD
GOVERNANCE

In explaining his concept, Johnston insists that the policy prescriptions of the past decade or so, including especially the push to worldwide free trade and communications, will be socially beneficial in the long run. But, he recalls, such major social upheavals as the French and Russian Revolutions invariably grew out of the people's perception that the benefits of progress were not being fairly shared. Necessary restructuring and efficiencies must, he insists, be applied with a sense for their immediate social consequences, and with an eye toward mobilising public support for globalisation. Joe Public must feel himself part of the process.

Johnston's emphasis on social justice will, inevitably, inflect the Organisation's thinking in a number of areas. It will not, however, revolutionise anything. As Johnston points out, most of the major projects initiated by his predecessor, Jean-Claude Paye – from the *Jobs Study* to the pioneering programme on age-ing – already concentrated on the interface between structural adjustment and social welfare. Indeed, though OECD is often thought of as a macroeconomic institution, it has been working steadily on social policy since the early 1960's.

Raiding the baker's, French Revolution (from Roger Viollet collection)

Soon after taking office, the Secretary-General laid down a number of specific policy markers to help the Organisation address the challenge he sees ahead. He calls for closer study of the effect of macroeconomic policy and microeconomic adjustments, with special attention to the potential trade-offs between employment and inflation. He asks for a critical look at the *speed* of public-sector downsizing, with emphasis on retraining, mobility and retirement policies. In the area of public investments, he argues the case for maintaining and extending infrastructures rather than leaving future generations to pay the bill.

Much of Johnston's thinking applies with special relevance to the world beyond the borders of his own organisation. Relations with the poor and the rapidly-enriching parts of the world have taken up more and more of OECD energies in recent years, and that is a trend that will continue. Johnston believes that the benefits of globalisation are, if anything, more promising for the developing countries than for those which already enjoy a high standard of living. At any rate, there is potential mutual gain.

Indeed, Johnston's view of the world's medium-term prospects, if nurtured by international co-operation, borders on the evangelical. In a speech delivered in Berlin, he declared: "I believe that we are on the threshold of a global revolution: that the benefits of a global market place, combined with effective international institutions, will set humanity on a course of increasing prosperity through technological innovation and societal evolution that we can only dare to dream of."

Donald Johnston, 1997

How to get there from here?

Certainly not easily. In the coming years, OECD will face a continuing budget crunch. To deal with it, Johnston launched a management reform that includes a measure of down-sizing and budget-paring. But the emphasis is on modern, flexible "objective-driven" management, eliminating waste, promoting managerial initiative. The horizontal approach to problem-solving will continue and will be extended. There will be a new emphasis on telling OECD's story to member governments, their populations and the world at large. Among Johnston's key objectives is a communications strategy that will make OECD more visible and that will counter "false perceptions of the negative implications of globalisation". He demonstrates his own commitment to one-on-one communication by inviting e-mail correspondence from the Organisation's staff at every level – and reading and answering it every day.

On a substantive level, the Organisation undertook a long, painstaking and ultimately crucial "prioritisation process" involving all its leading experts and managers. The objective: to set a broad agenda for work into the first two decades of the next century, weeding out secondary programmes and concentrating on those areas that are likely to offer the greatest policy challenges and opportunities to member governments.

Clearly, OECD membership is set to grow, but neither the pace of enlargement nor the list of prospective candidates is yet in hand. Most feel that OECD must reach out to non-members and bring some of them into the family. But everyone recognises the risks of losing focus and homogeneity if the process is pushed too fast. There is a variety of options for streamlining decision-making in the Council, but the consensus approach is highly valued by many members, especially the smaller ones, and will not be abandoned lightly.

OECD news conference, 1995

Change, then, in almost every area.

But there is a tradition to be nurtured, too. A tradition that underlies everything OEEC and OECD have been and done since the very beginning.

Generosity is at the root of that tradition, and a fundamental optimism about the human future, even in face of the horror of war. George Marshall incarnated the tradition, and his Plan demonstrated its practicability. Marshall's contemporaries and followers – Hoffman and Harriman, Robert Schuman and Jean Monnet, Charles de Gaulle and Konrad Adenauer, John Kennedy and Henry Kissinger, six distinguished Secretaries-General and thousands of devoted staffers – have carried it on.

Renewal, innovation, adaptation and even sharp shifts of strategy are inherent in OECD's mission and methodology. So are the custom of robust argument and back-breaking work, the furious activity that characterises virtually every day in the life of this château. The "rich countries' think tank", as it is known to both supporters and detractors, has its foibles, has made its mistakes. But it has played an irreplaceable role in this most eventful and successful half-century of human history.

It is ready to play that same role in the next.

Hall of OECD's Château

Robert Marjolin

René Sergent

Thorkil Kristensen

Emile van Lennep

Jean-Claude Paye

Donald Johnston

SECRETARIES-GENERAL, DEPUTIES AND ASSISTANTS SINCE 1948

OECD PERIOD

Secretaries-General
1996-	Donald J. Johnston (CAN)
1984-1996	Jean-Claude Paye (FR)
1969-1984	Emile van Lennep (NL)
1961-1969	Thorkil Kristensen (DNK)

Deputy Secretaries-General
1995-	Joanna S. Shelton (US)
1995-1996	Salvadore Zecchini (ITA)
1990-1996	Makoto Taniguchi (JAP)
1988-1995	Robert Cornell (US)
1985-1996	Pierre Vinde (SWE)
1980-1988	Jacob Myerson (US)
1980-1985	Paul Le Merle (FR)
1974-1980	Charles G. Wootton (US)
1970-1980	Gérard Eldin (FR)
1967-1973	Benson Lane Timmons (US)
1963-1967	Michael Harris (US)
1961-1970	Jean Cottier (FR)
1961-1966	Charles N. Adair (US)

Assistant Secretaries-General
1990-1995	Salvatore Zecchini (ITA)
1973-1975	Frederick J. Atkinson (UK)
1973-1975	Helmut Abramowski (GER)
1970-1973	Herbert Konig (GER)
1970-1974	Rinieri Paulucci di Calboli (ITA)
1967-1969	Walter F. Rau (GER)
1964-1966	Wilhelm Hanemann (GER)
1963-1973	Christopher R. Dow (UK)
1961-1964	Günter Keiser (GER)
1961-1970	Luciano Giretti (ITA)
1961-1967	Jack Downie (UK)

OEEC PERIOD

Secretaries-General
1953-1961	René Sergent (FR)
1948-1953	Robert Marjolin (FR)

Deputy Secretaries-General
	John Cahan (CAN)
	Henry J. B. Lintott (UK)
	Guido Colonna (ITA)

PERMANENT REPRESENTATIVES OF THE MEMBER COUNTRIES TO THE OECD AND OEEC

AUSTRALIA

1995-	Mr. Ralph Hillman
1993-1995	Mr. Trevor Boucher
1991-1993	Mr. David Borthwick
1988-1991	Mr. Ed Visbord
1985-1998	Mr. Alexander McGoldrick
1983-1985	Mr. Fred Argy, OBE
1980-1983	Mr. James Charles Humphreys
1977-1980	Mr. Francis Patrick Donovan
1973-1977	Mr. Roy Cameron
1971-1973	Sir Ronald Walker, CBE

AUSTRIA

1993-	Mr. Peter Jankowitsch
1982-1993	Mr. Georg Lennkh
1978-1982	Dr. Peter Jankowitsch
1968-1978	Dr. Carl Bobleter
1964-1968	Dr. Arno Halusa
1958-1964	Dr. Carl Bobleter
1949-1958	Mr. Herbert Prack

BELGIUM

1994-	Baron Hubert van Houtte
1991-1994	Mr. Theo L.R. Lansloot
1987-1991	Mr. Juan Cassiers
1986-1987	Mr. Guy Stuyck
1983-1986	Mr. Théo De Dobbeleer
1979-1983	Mr. Hervé Robinet
1975-1979	Mr. August Lonnoy
1974-1974	Mr. Herman Noppen
1953-1974	Mr. Roger Ockrent
1948-1953	Comte Hadelin de Meeus d'Argenteuil

CANADA

1995-	Mr. Kimon Valaskakis
1991-1995	Ms. Anne Marie Doyle
1988-1991	Mr. L. Michael Berry
1983-1988	Mr. William Jenkins
1980-1983	Mr. Randolph A. Gherson
1975-1980	Mr. Ronald Stuart MacLean
1972-1975	Mr. Peter Milburn Towe
1969-1972	Mr. James Russel McKinney
1965-1969	Mr. Charles John Small
1962-1965	Mr. James Conningsby Langley

CCE

1995-	Mr. Piergiorgio Mazzocchi
1988-1994	Mr. Raymond Phan Van Phi
1984-1988	Mr. Pierre Duchateau
1979-1984	Mr. Jean-Pierre Leng
1966-1979	Mr. Aldolphe de Baerdemaeker
1962-1966	Mr. Helmuth Cammann

CZECH REPUBLIC

1997-	Mr. Jaromir Privratsky

DENMARK

1992-	Mr. Torben Mailand Christensen
1991-1992	Mr. Gunnar Riberholdt
1989-1991	Mr. Jens Christensen
1986-1989	Mr. Henrik Netterstrom
1979-1986	Mr. Hans R. Tabor
1973-1979	Mr. Vagn Aage Korsbaek
1968-1973	Mr. Vagn Hoffmeyer Hoelgaard
1965-1967	Mr. Svend Aage Nielsen
1957-1965	Mr. Mathias Aagaard Wassard
1954-1956	Mr. Jens Anthon Vestbirk
01.04.1950- 31.01.1954	Mr. Eyvind Bartels
01.06.1948- 31.03.1950	Mr. Erling Kristiansen

FINLAND

1991-	Mr. Pasi Rutanen
1983-1991	Mr. Wilhelm Breitenstein
1978-1983	Mr. Pekka Malinen
1976-1978	Mr. Paul Gustaffson
1969-1976	Mr. Ralph Enckell
1968-1969	Mr. Richard R. Seppälä

FRANCE

1993-	Ms Marie-Claude Cabana
1991-1993	Mr. Jaques-Alain de Sédouy
1989-1991	Mr. Bernard Bochet
1987-1989	Mr. Marc Bonnefous
1982-1987	Mr. Emile Cazimajou
1978-1982	Mr. Christian d'Aumale
1975-1978	Mr. Jean-Marc Boegner
1965-1975	Mr. François Valéry

GERMANY

1996-	Dr. Werner Kaufmann-Bühler
1993-1996	Dr. Mario Graf von Matuschka
1985-1993	Dr. Klaus Meyer
1979-1985	Dr. Horst-Krafft Robert
1973-1979	Dr. Egon Emmel
1968-1973	Mr. Hans Carl Graf von Hardenberg
1964-1973	Dr. Rudolf Vogel
1961-1963	Dr. Carl H. Mueller-Graaf
1951-1961	Dr. Karl Werkmeister
1949-1951	Dr. H. Karl Mangoldt-Reibholdt

GREECE

1996-	Mr. Spyros Lioukas
1994-1995	Ms Kalliope Nikolaou
1991-1993	Mr. Dimitrios Germidis
1986-1990	Mr. Dimitris Koulourianos
1982-1985	Pr. Argyris A. Fatouros
1981-1982	Mr. Constantin Stavrou
1974-1981	Mr. Dimitri Athanassopoulos
1972-1974	Mr. Jean Apostilidis
1956-1971	Mr. Theodore Christidis
1953-1956	Mr. Leandros Nicolaïdis
1949-1953	Mr. Alexandre Verdelis

HUNGARY

1996-	Mr. Làszlò Balogh

ICELAND

1994-	Mr. Sverri Haukur Gunnlaugsson
1989-1993	Mr. Albert Gudmundsson
1985-1989	Mr. Haraldur Kröyer
1982-1985	Mr. Tomas Armann Tomasson
1976-1982	Mr. Einar Benediktsson
1965-1976	Mr. Henrik Sv. Björnsson
1962-1965	Mr. Petur Thorsteinsson
1956-1961	Mr. Hans G. Andersen
1948-1956	Mr. Petur Benediktsson

IRELAND

1995-	Mr. Patrick O'Connor
1991-1995	Mr. John H. F. Campbell
1987-1991	Mr. Tadhg O'Sullivan
1986-1987	Mr. Andrew O'Rourke
1981-1986	Mr. Brendan Dillon
1970-1974	Mr. Hugh J. McCann
	Mr. Eammon Lucas Kennedy
1966-1970	Mr. Thomas Vincent Commins

ITALY

1997-	Mr. Alessandro Vattani
1993-1997	Mr. Pietro Calamia
1988-1993	Mr. Luigi Fontana Giusti
1986-1988	Mr. Ferdinando Salleo
1983-1986	Mr. Giuseppe Jacoangeli
1980-1983	Mr. Marco Francisci di Baschi
1978-1980	Mr. Fausto Bacchetti
1973-1978	Mr. Luciano Conti
1972-1973	Mr. Pinna Caboni
1969-1972	Mr. Francesco Cavalletti di Oliveto Sabino
1965-1968	Mr. Raimondo Manzini
1961-1965	Mr. Casto Caruso
1956-1961	Mr. Guiseppe Cosmelli
1955-1956	Mr. Leonardo Vitetti
1948-1955	Mr. Attilio Cattani

JAPAN

1995-	Mr. Masaji Takahashi
1992-1995	Mr. Yoshiyasu Sato
1989-1992	Mr. Hiroaki Fujii
1988-1989	Mr. Hisashi Owada
1984-1988	Mr. Hiromu Fukada
1982-1984	Mr. Reishi Teshima
1980-1982	Mr. Hiromichi Miyazaki
1975-1980	Mr. Tsuyoshi Hirahara
1972-1975	Mr. Bunroku Yoshino
1970-1972	Mr. Kiyohiko Tsurumi
1967-1970	Mr. Tadao Kato
1964-1967	Mr. Haruki Mori

KOREA

1996	Mr. Bohn Young Koo

LUXEMBOURG

1992-	Mr. Paul Mertz
1984-1991	Mr. Pierre Wurth
1978-1984	Mr. André Philippe
1971-1978	Mr. Camille Dumont
1967-1971	Mr. Georges Heisbourg
1959-1967	Mr. Paul Reuter
1952-1959	Mr. Nicholas Hommel

MEXICO

1994-	Mr. Carlos Hurtado

NETHERLANDS

1996-	Mr. Egbert F. Jacobs
1991-1996	Mr. Ferdinand van Dam
1986-1991	Mr. Anton G.O. Smitsendonk
1983-1986	Mr. Franz Italianer
1977-1983	Mr. Will F. Pelt
1974-1977	Mr. Klaus Westerhoff
1969-1974	Mr. Johan Kaufmann
1967-1969	Mr. Jan Strengers
1961-1967	Mr. Han N. Boon

NEW ZEALAND

1995-	Mr. Richard Woods
1992-1995	Mr. Christopher David Beeby
1987-1991	Ms Judith C. Trotter
1982-1987	Mr. John G. McArthur
1979-1982	Mr. John Vivian Scott
1975-1979	Mr. John G. McArthur
1973-1975	Mr. Owston Paul Gabites

NORWAY

1994-	Mr. Per Martin ølberg
1989-1994	Mr. Bjørn Barth
1986-1989	Mr. Thorvald Moe
1977-1986	Mr. Jens Mogens Boyesen
1974-1976	Mr. Georg Kristiansen
1973-1973	Mr. Sigurd Trygve Ekeland
1968-1973	Mr. Rolf Fredrik Hancke
1964-1967	Mr. Georg Kristiansen
1955-1964	Mr. Jens Mogens Boyesen
1949-1955	Mr. Arne Skaug

POLAND

1996-	Mr. Mieczyslaw SZOSTAK (*ad interim*)

PORTUGAL

1996-	Mr. Jorge de Lemos Godinho
1993-1996	Mr. José António da Silveira Godinho
1988-30.10.1992	Mr. Fernando Augusto dos Santos Martins
1981-1988	Mr. Pedro Manuel Cruz Roseta
1979-1981	Mr. Henrique Granadeiro
1974-1979	Mr. Manuel de Almeida Bello
1971-1974	Mr. Joao Rodrigues Simoes Affra
1970-1971	Mr. Joao Freitas Cruz
1967-1970	Mr. Joao de Deus Battaglia Ramos
1964-1967	Dr. José Manuel Fragosco Dr. José Calvet de Magelliaes

SPAIN

1996-	Mr. José Luis Feito
1993-1996	Mr. Claudio Aranzadi
1990-1993	Mr. Eloy Ybañez
1987-1990	Mr. José Antonio Lopez Zaton
1983-1986	Mr. José-Vicente Torrente Secorun
1978-1983	Mr. Tomas Chavarri y del Rivero
1974-1978	Mr. Francisco Javier Vallaure y Fernandez-Peña
1970-1973	Mr. Francisco Javier Elorza y Echaniz Marquis de Nerva
1965-1970	Mr. José Aragonés Vila
1958-1964	Mr. José Nuñez Iglesias

SWEDEN

1995-	Mr. Anders Ferm
1991-1995	Mr. Staffan Sohlman
1985-1991	Mr. Bo Kjellén
1976-1985	Mr. Hans E.O. Colliander
1972-1976	Mr. Leif Belfrage
1964-1972	Mr. Carl Henrik von Platen
1953-1963	Mr. Sten Ingemar Richardsson-Hägglöf
1949-1953	Mr. Erik von Sydow

SWITZERLAND

1995-	Mr. Jean-Pierre Zehnder
1988-1994	Mr. Eric Roethlisberger
1983-1988	Mr. Jean Zwahlen
1974-1983	Mr. Albert Grübel
1969-1974	Mr. Marcel Heimo
1967-1969	Mr. Claude Caillat
1957-1966	Mr. Agostino Soldati
1953-1957	Mr. Gérard Bauer

TURKEY

1995-	Mr. Orhan Güvenen
1990-1994	Mr. Temel Iskit
1988-1990	Dr. Mustafa Asula
1983-1988	Mr. Tansug Bleda
1981-1983	Mr. Pertev Subasi
1972-1981	Mr. Memduh Aytür
1970-1972	Mr. Kamurah Gürün
1968-1970	Mr. Metin Kizickaya
1965-1968	Mr. Cahit Kayra
1962-1964	Mr. Münir Mostar
1961-1962	Prof. Aziz Köklo
1952-1961	Mr. Melmet Ali Tiney

OECD PUBLICATIONS, 2, rue André-Pascal, 75775 PARIS CEDEX 16
PRINTED IN FRANCE
(03 97 04 1 P) ISBN 92-64-15503-1 – No. 49445 1997
© OECD 1997